OCTOBER

A novel

William Auten

FIRE IN HAND MEDIA

October
First edition
©2021 William Auten

All rights reserved. No part of this book may be used, reproduced, or transmitted in any form or by electronic or mechanical means, including photocopying, recording, or any information storage or retrieval system, without written permission from the publisher except in cases of brief quotations in critical articles, reviews, social media, and noncommercial uses.

No responsibility for loss caused to any individual or organization acting on or refraining from action as a result of the material in this publication can be accepted by the author or Fire In Hand Media.

This book is a work of fiction. All characters, dialogues, scenes, and situations are either products of the author's imagination or used fictitiously. Any resemblance to actual events, locales, or persons living or dead is coincidental.

ISBN (print): 9780578866536
ISBN (ebook): 9780578866574

Published by Fire in Hand Media
Fire In Hand Media colophon is a registered trademark of Fire In Hand Media LLC
fireinhand.com

OCTOBER

1

This morning I find myself standing in front of closed curtains and in the gaps of twos—two months, two days, two lights, two images. Spots on my eyes from deep sleep burst and fade. My dream lingers in this room, and for several seconds, the ghostlike shapes that danced in front of me slough off into remaining darkness. Behind the curtains, a thin band of fire breaks up the bottom of black sky, summer continues its tilt into fall, and the first of October has come on as easily as a foot steps in front of the other. September was just over there, near my computer, where evening and morning swap, and where I stand in the middle, no longer asleep but awfully sleepy inside echoes of who and what I saw. Dawn is well on its way. Everything is finding its place on either side of the curtains.

No blood on my head. No pain there, my neck, or anywhere—at least no new pain from standing here, which will probably give me some pain later today. By lunchtime, my ankles will bulge like summer ticks. My hands—as arthritic and spotted as they were yesterday and as arthritic and spotted for the new day and new month. Nothing significant around me has changed. My apartment is quiet. My things have not shifted—books, bills, notes to myself, or mementos, especially Ray's cane. The streets behind the curtains are quiet. Cole has not caved in or broken apart overnight—no flooding, no power outages, no surprise storms. The mountains have not crumbled into the foothills, which have not smothered the Tri-Valley. The early morning air seeping through the desk's window, which leaks regardless of the season, chills me.

I tighten my robe. The curtains' navy slightly brightens. The clock by my computer does not reassure me I have stood here for only a little bit. But how long? I don't recall sleepwalking, but anything seems possible nowadays now I'm my parents' age. Mom always worried Dad would end up in the middle of downtown Cole—not worried he'd die from traffic or a bite from a rabid animal but he'd be standing wide open on Main Street in his pajamas, and the town, having watched Dad make the journey, wouldn't bother stopping him, most of them probably waving at him. "Hiya, Marvin. Would you like a cup of coffee?" None of them would do anything else but fix their breakfast, get ready for their day, and have some new gossip, especially for church.

The dream I had before I shuffled from my bedroom, across the living room, and to my computer belongs now to the past. I chased a shadow never revealing its source, but as soon as I reached it, it split like smoke. "So vivid," Dad said about his dreams. "Everyone I knew alive and dead visited me at some point. I guess they had something important to tell me or just

OCTOBER

wanted to shoot the breeze before they had to go back. I was never scared, not even with Cousin Ralph who smelled like his favorite bottle. I never had much to tell them or to give anything to them before they left."

Maybe the house woke me. Maybe its old bones needed some attention from me, wanted me to make sure my old bones would fill its chairs and rooms, occupy it again. "Patty," its old walls and joints whispered. As long as I've been in one of its apartments, I reckon it doesn't want me to leave and, if it held more than memories and moments and made a home for me, if it had arms and hands, it might do all it can to keep me from drifting too far.

Maybe I got up in the middle of the night because I convinced myself, in my hours of sleeping, Saul sent another note to me, or maybe two, and his message, many hours ago when the moon shone behind the curtains, was not definitive and abrupt. After our chat ended, I went to bed convinced I would not hear from him again. His promise of a translation for his photo was the only new thing from him. I turned off my computer, wiped my eyes, and accepted that was that between us as I pulled the bedspread over me and whispered, as I do every night, "Goodnight. I love and miss you" to Ray.

If I had never met Saul back in February and answered him, if I had never pursued him on those cold nights or up until last night, I may still be sound asleep. My computer holds Saul's photo, his many promises, and our conversations. Standing here, did I want to see myself arrive from the past and sit in the desk chair, turn on the computer, and stare at ourselves in the monitor? Had Patty arrived from the past, would I have asked her who watches the living? The night? The dead? The day? The sky, with or without sun or with or without stars, connecting the living and the dead?

Every time my computer starts, the first thing to load is Ray's image of us standing at the mountain cabin many years ago, which fills me with joy, love, and sadness. But Saul is also there, and his photo pushes me away as much as it pulls me back. His photo stung me the first time, and it has answered me without me asking it any questions. When Saul's photo consumes me, I panic because of Ray, which often wakes me in the middle of the night because I have misplaced something about our life together, like a map missing one of its paths.

Avoiding anything about Saul is impossible. While I wait at the microwave for popcorn, I glance at the computer screen. His photo flickers when I take off my makeup in the bathroom and stare at the mirror. Getting ready for bed, I pull back the covers, and streetlights outside my apartment or the curtains glowing with moonshine halos the desk.

I've sometimes imagined Saul's photo would change during the months it sat in my computer, or if I didn't think about the photo or his promise of a translation, everything about him and us would go away. Maybe a gnome-like creature would emerge

OCTOBER

from the digital universe, crawl into the folder, and push around the pixels and nudge the tones until his photo held something different than when I received it and reminded me where I was and was to be. Sometimes I wish his photo would disappear from my computer or maybe today will be the day my computer doesn't start, but then I regret wishing Saul and his image would go away and I never met him.

Chatting with him has not been complicated or too confusing. We described ourselves and what we were doing when we were online. We have never followed through on meeting in person. It's never been about that. Anything more would require work and energy beyond what we put in. We're limited to who we are and can't become. And I made it clear to him where I was with it. He has lost a spouse, but unlike me, he has been willing to start fresh with love and dating.

He never once said to me I could trust him, which, as far as I'm concerned, someone says in order to get something out of you, and trust loses what it's meant to bring out. I have never seen his face nor heard his voice. He has fulfilled all his promises to me in the past, writing to me whenever our schedule fleshed out on its own. We became familiar with our habits, likes and dislikes, and our secrets. From a distance, wherever he was, neither space nor time separated us. He claimed he was states away, but he was in the same room with me—no longer strangers.

His photo arrived like a door dropped between the past and future. I have never sent him a photo of any kind. He's never asked for one of me. I cannot confirm what he said to me has been the truth. But I also cannot confirm what he said to me has been lies.

Every day, I move between Saul's image and Ray's. And although Ray has been gone for a while and I live alone, I am never alone because he and our images when we were together and Saul and his image have me. One photo greets me, like a face in a crowd, and the other image, more familiar over time, also comes and goes. Both photos have been with me at peaks, in valleys, and on the plains in between. I pass by them daily and nightly, month to month, but I should only have one.

. . .

Before the end of September, Saul wrote <Let me send this photo to you. It's beautiful because of its silence and colors. And that setting. Wow. Just wait. I got it on a trip I took with a friend. I had this old camera of mine I had not used in a while. I dusted it off and took it with me. And am I glad I did! Lots of good pictures on that trip but this one. Boy oh boy. Really jolted me like an ice cold bath thrown atop you, fire held under your feet, and an electric shock all at the same time.>

<That's a lot!>

OCTOBER

<It sure is, but it hits home you know? It's got to in some ways. Otherwise it ain't doing a lick of good! Those tones and what's inside. One of those notions you don't want to deal with but we all have to when the time comes. And it will. For every one of us. Don't matter who you are or what you look like.>

The cursor on his end stopped and, after a few seconds, started blinking again.

<I want to share it with you. Maybe you could get something out of it. I bet my bottom dollar you will. I needed it. You need it. Heck we all need it.>

<You're so thoughtful. Thank you. I can't wait to see it.>

<There's an inscription on the base of the main stone in the middle of the photo right there at the front. My friend who was with me is working on the translation of the phrase. She's good with that kind of stuff. When I get it I'll send it to you. Talk to you soon. Goodnight.>

I didn't ask about this "she" he mentioned, but he sent the image and the promise, and then the end of September came and went. Many weeks and days of silence have added up, and Saul has said nothing about why he has stopped talking to me—nothing about his circumstances or a predicament stopping him from logging on at the same time when we used to. No more messages. No more spending nights together. No more sharing. I have sent him something small to him every few days. <Hi> <I miss talking with you.> <How have you been? Would love to talk

to you when you have time. Hope all is well.> <I hope you're all right. Please let me know if there's anything I can do.> <If someone you love is in trouble or in poor health, I know what that's like. And you know that.> <Would love to hear from you. Davis and Karen had quite a day today, and I heard all about it. The season sure is changing.>

Maybe he needed space. Maybe I was pushy or confused myself with who and where we were. Maybe he got bored. He isn't obligated to talk to me, and he certainly doesn't have to keep up anything or follow through on anything. Maybe things in life are made for lasting long enough before they have to break down. I have to keep in mind Saul has his own life, separate from mine, and his words can be like rumors of good weather or birds folks around Cole and the Tri-Valley know about and can only describe because they appear on their own time, often out of nowhere.

. . .

Save for the gray sky, which in the background is nearly white in spots and spreads over a field, Saul's photo is black and white. All the other details are degrees of black. The grass is gray. Many stones crowd the ground and touch the air. When I first saw Saul's photo, the sky and the single stone underneath the sky were the only things visible to me. He sent it after I told him about Ray. His photo told me a little at first, but after seeing it many times, it tells me things I knew but had forgotten.

OCTOBER

Not every photo tells the same story, but the place in Saul's looks less like a place and more a story everyone knows. Similar places in other parts of the world hold a similar message in fields like his photo. Some photos tell about beginnings, some tell about ends, and some tell about everything in the middle. But his photo talks about beginnings and ends. What's left in the middle are stones reminding folks to be ready—not for a harsh winter or the return of spring and inclement weather but for some other upcoming time and place where stones, standing like sentinels under the sky, recall us.

His camera didn't capture all the gravestones in the graveyard —just the one he sent to me. In the background, several other markers pile up like stones brightened by the sun in shallow water. I don't know the person buried, and Saul doesn't either, but in a way, we know. The cross leans a little to the left but not because of Saul's unsteady hand. It is old enough it sinks into the ground, or the ground, being older, has sunk more as time wears it down. The horizon flattens behind the cross—no hills, no mountains, no trees. Faded are the dates and names on the marker, save for the inscription in the foreground of the one cross he focused on. The time in the photo could be anytime with the sun out—morning, noon, afternoon. The base of the cross in Saul's photo is the only gravestone with writing, and although the words of the dead are in a foreign language, I understand them—distant and near and when they were here among us.

• • •

A letter sits alongside his photo inside a folder on my computer.

Dear Saul,

I reach out to you because I hope you will reach back. The only thoughts on my mind have been when I will hear from you again.

You understand what I've gone through because you've gone through it too. More importantly you have been there for me when others haven't.

Remember when we confused the time, our different time zones, and you thought you would be late for an appointment in the morning you had? Remember when we talked about meeting in St. Louis, Nashville, or Richmond, one of those river cities close to us and one I've wanted to go to, or maybe a city between us, like Atlanta or New Orleans? We talked about walking with ice-cream cones in hand, people-watching, and sitting on a park bench and waiting for the sunset. We talked about going to venues to hear live music. I have daydreamed about weekend drives or long hikes along a river, about cooking pork loins with bacon wrapped around them. I can do those things without you, but I also don't want to do them without you.

Why haven't I heard from you? Why are you silent with me, so much a stranger you avoid me? We used to talk long into

OCTOBER

the night. Why can't we have more than silence? I love Ray, I still love Ray, but I need you.

I have missed you for so long now I am embarrassed by my loneliness and am ashamed for reaching out to you to help me take it away. You said loss and the need to somehow walk with it is so great and necessary to people. It's like a road we have to walk especially when we don't feel like moving. When you said this, it was like a bell chiming for the first time in a long time.

For a long time, I felt guilty because my time with Ray faded away as my time with you grew. And yet I cannot walk away from an old life and into a new one without memories pushing and pulling me in different directions, sometimes even dragging me with what I once had. When I remember our times, and I see what you've shared with me, why I was drawn to you rushes back to me. I do not regret becoming close with you. I did not go looking for you, but I also could not have stopped it. It was inevitable.

I want to know what you want. Do you want me in your life? Do you want me only when you want me? You must know I want you in my life. At what capacity? I don't know, but I am sure I miss you. My loneliness cannot bear you not being in my life. I don't want to be alone. With my life before you, I know I am not, but at the same time, without you, I am. I miss my friend.

I have yet to send this letter. I go to my words but then turn from them. They wait for their own time. I have to remind myself, with Saul being a ghost, not having a response is a response to a question I ask daily.

If I could keep Saul's photo but lose him forever, I don't think I would. If I could have back Saul the friend and lose his photo, I would. The two are attached, but I have the photo and only the specter of the friend. His photo takes me in, but I am always outside. I find myself turning around inside the photo, and as I do, I turn around inside the image—among the sky, grass, and stones. But I also have to keep moving.

I don't know if the translation he promised will arrive. I have checked my computer nearly every day for it. The grave's inscription holds the words while I hold the photo, and I have to wait for the translation to reveal more than its stone surface. It's like waiting for two messages to arrive simultaneously—one for then and one for now.

Were Saul to reach out to me and want to pick up where we left off, I wouldn't say no, but I also wouldn't say yes. He has those parts of me I shared with him. He made me feel like whatever I had in my hands to offer was enough. To say nothing to him, to cut our conversations from my life never crossed my mind until recently. He helped me see the absence of anything physical and the presence of everything else. I left one reality in order to talk with Saul, and I face it again when I reappear. I confided things in him I had confided in a handful of people, including Ray. Part of me says I should move so far from Saul returning would be like a fool stepping into water flooding the only road under the horizon.

OCTOBER

...

Other faces and places haunt me. They move in the background, foreground, or alongside me, especially the computer's desktop photo of Ray and me at the mountain's cabin from years ago. He bought the computer for work, but when his job provided a better one, it became ours at our home. I told Saul I sold that house and any items my apartment or storage couldn't hold, but I couldn't let the computer go despite it's well past its prime and would be a laughed at outside my apartment's walls. As much as Ray disliked being on it, I can't update it. "I don't want to be plugged in like that," he said. He gave it to both of us, but it became mine.

<The same computer you're using to chat with me?> Saul asked me one night.

<The one and the same.>

<Hot diggity dog. I am one lucky guy. When my first wife died the refuse truck rolled up and took away several pounds of memories I had not touched or seen for so long. It was a purging before starting over. A few things of Courtney's I wanted back once the truck left but having a "business attitude" kept me in check until my heart told me the things leaving had nothing to do about "profit" and had everything to do about a very different "bottom line," if you catch my drift.>

<I do. Very much so.>

I love seeing Ray and me in the cabin photo. It whispers to me what we went through when we disappeared for a week from our life in Cole before having to return to it. It holds the good and the bad of a time spent with his body and my body and their changes. The doctors were cautiously optimistic when also reminding us about reality, saying anything like a vacation would help Ray alleviate, not eradicate, his cancer. Good illusions are better than bad ones, and if you're going to be part of an illusion, then it better be the good ones because they aren't lying to you in order to hold something over you, to take something from you, or to control you. The good illusions want to bring happiness and joy like a magic trick. And, when I'm at the computer, Ray greets and says goodbye to me, even after spending time with Saul.

That mountain cabin was a splurge, and it took in our hopes and fears. It had a life of its own—squawking, squeaking, rattling, like my apartment. It breathed when we breathed. No snow or cold rain ever fell when we were there. Sun filled our days with warmth and light. At night, the temperatures dropped, and in our bed, Ray and I were close again emotionally and physically. The whole week was like the old times we had when he was the old Ray. We fixed breakfasts, lunches, and dinners. We watched movies. We read. He wrote letters to his kids and family. We hiked around the lake. He did the dishes, helped cut vegetables and meats. Not once did he cry out for me. Not once did he wake up in a sweat and ask for water or help. Everything Ray did in the

OCTOBER

cabin and in those mountains was a small victory. He made his cane on that trip and brought it home until I had to sell our house and carry his cane to my apartment, setting it in the corner behind my computer and in front of the curtains. Ray's cane overshadows all the mementos from our old house. He cut away everything not a tree limb—and did with a determination I had not seen in so long. I'm glad I didn't send him into the other world with it and, instead, kept it so I could see it before I leave the house or when I sit in the living area with day or night pouring through the curtains.

If the rocks near the cabin and on that mountain top from that week could tell a story, they would say how close they are to the sky, much closer than other rocks here in the Tri-Valley or Cole, and anyone or anything standing or moving on them is closer to the sky than they were down there with the rest of them. If the rocks in Saul's photo could tell a story, they would say how far away they are from the sky yet are doing all they can to reach it and to be seen by it. Weather shaped the rocks in Ray's photo. In Saul's photo, hands carved the rocks marking points along a path starting in dust, reaching a limit, and returning to the ground.

Ray wanted something as clear as water or a cloudless sky brightened by a never-setting sun. I wanted nothing more than to walk from the cabin with him, to the lake, and across the mountain face and all its rocks, stones, peaks, and dips, deeply into the trees, and with the labor needed to love more than the people attached to moments not lasting past a single day. I wished for no one else to be with then, and I wish for no one else to be with now. Saul not being in my life saddens me in a way I have not felt since Ray died, which bothers me because I still very much love Ray and will forever be married to him. I don't care what some of the checkboxes say when I fill out forms. I married Ray, he married me, and I am still married to Ray, and as far as I'm concerned, he's still married to me.

• • •

Earlier this year, on Valentine's Day, of all days, I joined an online group interested in music. I had put off another New Year's resolution of "getting yourself out there," as my friend Gloria cheered me on, years after Ray. I didn't devote much time at first. Being online here or there on nights or weekends was enough.

Oldies But Goodies was the group's name. Saul was Blackbird918. He posted quite a bit about different bands, his opinions about them and their music, of which he provided plenty, and where and what these bands were up to now.

<Mostly Vegas acts or holiday specials, like Fourth of July or state fairs.>

<State fairs are the best.>

<Then we are two peas in a pod.>

OCTOBER

<Have you been to Vegas?>

<I can't say.>

<Why not?>

<What happens there stays there. Besides I am a Southern gentleman till the day I die.>

All of us online joked we had seen our favorite bands of days gone by at these kinds of events and we loved every minute of their performances. <They still got it!> we all wrote in agreement. <Mostly> we sometimes wrote. <They look like us. We look like them. If you get too close, you'll see the plastic surgery!>. Saul added encyclopedic knowledge without sounding stuffy. He talked about minor keys and how something was missing, which is why we listen to them.

Had Ray been around for this, he would have signed up as J. Sebastian Coltrane Bach, his two favorite musicians. He and I had private concerts in our living room listening to albums—everything from country to blues, jazz and rock, classical. Those songs lined our shelves, and almost every Friday dinner was devoted to playing them and sitting back with food and drinks in hand. "Spending time together, you and me here, enjoying life this way," he said, "one day our future selves will thank us for this." Before we married, he considered a music career. His father played in a jazz and gospel group in the area's bars and churches. His mother had a powerful voice. Ray sang several times for me when we dated—popular songs, old-timey songs—and when we were serious about each other, wrote "Patty Starts with a P." When he said the title, I nearly spit out my drink. He had no guitar and sang, "Patty starts with a P/And wherever she goes, she takes me/If she were to leave/I'd be so blue/And then her name would not be what I knew." When he was finished, I wiped my eyes from laughing and crying at the same time. He sang it to me one night after I had finished my shift at the library. He had a picnic with him, but rain snuck up on us that day and forced us into the break room. Several of my coworkers heard him, and they thought tonight would be the night he proposed, but it was only the song. But it was my song, and his silhouette sang in the cabin's kitchen on our trip to the mountains.

One of my first posts to the online group mentioned listening over and over to "God Only Knows" by the Beach Boys when Ray lay in a hospital bed after coughing up blood from relapsing. I said its lyrics and melody made me calm and didn't erase those bad moments in life but did shine a light on them until they were no longer shadows to avoid but to walk through.

<Shadows are made from a light present but not seen.> Saul responded.

<That's real good. Thank you.> I quickly replied.

<When I was a teen I thought that song was a sappy love song, but then my first serious girlfriend Leslie and I danced to it outside my old car I paid for in cash from all my after-school hours working at a machine shop.>

OCTOBER

<My heart be still! Not some spoiled college kid who was handed everything.>

<Not me in a million years. She later married someone else, but I realized how much I loved her, no matter where we were or who we had become. She secretly agrees with this still to this day.>

<Do you stay in touch with her?>

<You better bet your last dollar on that. All of them.>

<"All of them?">

<Too many to count!>

<How many?>

<We have this unspoken understanding between us. If things were different, if this were some other time and place, some other world or dimension, like I keep reading about on the science sites, we'd be together hands down. But not to be. She's with someone else and that's OK. I can say I never once cheated on her.>

<Well, aren't you a Boy Scout!>

<Not always but I do my best.>

Conservations like this between us went on until moderators reminded us to keep things focused on the topic pertinent to the group or to take it offline. I found myself sitting in my chair by my desk, my hands over the keyboard, staring out the curtains or, if they were closed, through them, and wondering what Saul was doing or if he was online until Ray's cane leaning in the corner behind the computer caught my eye. I'd try not to hurry home to jump on the computer first thing, but if I was close by when I heard a message ping, I ran to it and looked for his words, be they a question, a confirmation, or even a simple <Y> for yes, <N> for no, or <IDK> for I don't know. He used Internet slang more than I did. I joked with him either he was younger or hipper than me. <Both> he replied and threw in <LOL> and a cartoon smiley face wearing sunglasses. <Someday you'll find out. I promise.> Saul and I exchanged emails, and after that, we were by ourselves. We never returned to the group. No one from there asked where we had gone or if we were coming back or said we were missed. We joked about calling ourselves the only members of the Lonely Hearts Club.

<What's your real name?> he asked one night. <What do you really go by?>

<PVLP isn't good enough for you anymore?>

<Now we're rogue? No ma'am. Not your handle on here in our little corner of the Web. Your real one, please.>

<Pat.>

<Pat could be a guy or gal.>

<Patty.>

<Just Patty?>

<That's all you get for now.>

<I'm going to go out on a limb here and say you're really Patricia.>

OCTOBER

<Maybe.>

<I knew it.>

<LOL.>

<Look at you using that.>

<I'm a fast learner.>

<I knew that from day one.>

<My initials are PVLP.>

<And?>

<Patricia Vidalia Lee Pemberton.>

<That's beautiful.>

<Thank you. I prefer Patty because Patricia would mean the person saying my full first name needs me to hand over something than simply give it.>

<Too formal?>

<Yes. I feel this way the most when I fill out forms, wait in an office, or holding for customer service. When I first moved in here, my neighbors Davis and Karen called me "Patricia" because they had accidentally received some of my mail. I do not want to think what waits for me inside those typed envelopes, especially after Ray and anything doing with his family.>

<What's with his family?>

<I haven't talked to them in years.>

<That's tough.>

<Yes, we're getting through it.>

<It takes time.>

I had to stand up and get some water. Darkness from the rest of my apartment could not reach into the halo around my computer, and my kitchen's nightlight was bright enough to break up any of the darkness overflowing from my bedroom and the gray patches floating between its door and the path to my desk and chair, the front door, and the sidewalk rolling to the road I stopped walking because I had no hands to hold other than my own. The computer's glow opened like wings. Another message pinged as I turned to the sink and stopped the water after it spilled over.

<You still there?> Saul wrote.

<I had to get a drink.>

<I'm driving you to the bottle I'm this boring?>

<Ha. No. Water.>

<Phew but you'll have to pee, which means leaving me again. Use BRB in the future.>

<?>

<Be Right Back. I use it when I have to pee.>

I laughed and set the glass in front of me on the desk, and the water took in light from Ray's walking stick and Saul's words. <When I hear the name Patty, I think of someone wanting me, not a thing I have. I have been Patty for a long time, but it still feels like a new name. When I hear my name, I look forward to a moment waiting to be shared.>

<I like that.>

OCTOBER

<I used to go by Patricia when I was younger. It's a family name on Dad's side dating back to when Patricia Trimble and Robert Essen met in Jackson before moving to Guyton on the verge of the American Revolution. Mom's grandmother was Louisa Vidalia (née Meyer), and she was born and raised in Young County, three counties southeast near the foothills and the Chickataw River. Through family documents and my own research, I know quite a bit about her.>

<Genealogy is like a Tolkien story.>

<Full of darkness and dragons and paths winding into thickets and trouble?>

<Yes *and* goodness and guides for the goodness and paths winding out of trouble and into bigger history and less thorny spaces.>

<The good is hidden?>

<It has to be revealed because we cover it up. We forget it when making our own little histories about ourselves. But boy oh boy all those roots and limbs making a tree you can climb, swing from, or hold onto on a bad or a wonderful day. Walk right up to it. It has no choice but to take you in.>

Ray would have said something like that. I stood to refill my glass, but I also closed my eyes inside peace given to me by someone who was feeling less and less like a stranger. <Great Grandma Lou was a strong woman who bore seven children and fought off her family's illness better than the country doctor

whose split his services and knowledge between treating humans and farm animals. Mom said G.G. Lou soaked her kids in dirt an hour every day so they would toughen up quicker than any city children who had access to hospitals and medicine.>

<Country folk are way tougher and more resourceful than city folk.>

<That is true. And I'm living proof.>

<Same as a pie tin.>

<G.G. Lou would hand out books, pens, and papers to them for reading, writing, and drawing. They were on their own until she told them it was time to come in the house and clean up. She lined her sons and daughters up, not by age, height, or her favorites but in alphabetical order, before calling them out one by one. In my memory box, I have a photo of her. I do not look a thing like her, save for the thick curls of hair, which I cannot tell in the original if hers are black or dark brown. Her eyes, though, cut through fog. They must have been ice blue. My eyes blend in with olive-gray shadows. Her curls are tied up in a bun. I wear mine so short they're tight like pieces of shaved lumber on the ground.>

<You sound beautiful.>

My hands slid off the keyboard as I leaned back and stared at my reflection in the computer screen. I wanted to look from but could leave neither my reflection nor Saul. I almost teased him he had no idea; I had fooled him real good, thanks to the power of

OCTOBER

the Internet; or he was a few sheets to the wind—all of this while Ray's smile and voice tugged me. The cursor at the end of Saul's compliment blinked like a light over a door. I finished my glass of water and took a few seconds before continuing. <Thank you. That's always nice to hear.>

<You're welcome. And now back to our regular scheduled program...>

After blushing, I typed <G.G. Lou wears no makeup in that photo. Wrinkles weigh down her face, which mine are doing more and more these days. An ivory brooch clinches the lace around her neck. She has a stern look while she rests her hand on Great Grandpa Buford's shoulder. He sits in a wood chair and has a gun, its stock on the floor, resting between them. They are dressed in the finest suit and dress of the day a postman and a schoolteacher in Cole could afford. I like to safely assume neither G.G. Bu nor G.G. Lou cared much about fashion. They had other things on their minds to focus on.>

<They sure did. Sounds a lot like my families. Spitting image.>

<Patricia stuck with me until I turned thirteen when I announced to my parents I was to be called Patty, a precocious teenager who would rather read books than listen to music or watch television and who would someday be on the cover of magazines for discovering something new or shedding light on something or someone in a part of the world not everyone in

Cole knew about. The Tri-Valley, from DeMint to Taylor, would know about me. This first version of Patty also stopped calling her parents Mom and Dad and started calling them Marvin and Lee.>

<You got rebel blood in you using your parents' names!>

<When Ray and I married, my last name changed, and although we handed each other new lives and a new name for me, I kept everything else I had inherited up to that point, especially my many names and its roots.>

<Your name is a real good name. It's a mouthful. But a mouthful of sweet tea and honey biscuits. I like it a lot. I'm so pleased to meet you with that name.>

His cursor didn't blink for several minutes. <Are you really a gal? Your profile back at Oldies said you are, but this is the Internet.>

<As cold as the north wind blows, I swear I am. Are you really a guy?>

<My ex-wives can tell you real quick LOL. Joking about the exes but not really. Yes I am.>

<What's your full real name?>

<Saul Martin Gentry. My mom is the Martin. My dad was there when we liberated one of the Nazi camps. A man he got to know after the war was Saul Blankfein. A survivor and a good man. Real good man. Our families stayed in touch over many years. We were all at his funeral. We took care of his wife and

OCTOBER

kids. Lots of stories. I am named after him. I'm named after a man from the Tribe of Moses in the Old Testament. How about them apples? I reckon it all connects anyway. Besides I could change my name to Paul just like the story in the Gospels. Old Testament Part 2 as I like to call it.>

<What do you look like?>

<Big, burly man with thick bristly hair shocked white as cotton. My voice belongs in a choir's baritone section. Woodchips curl by my feet because I enjoy carving which balances the collection of fast cars sitting in a stand-alone garage on my property. They look so fast they go nowhere. I love my baseball cards, even the ones I never made any money with which is pretty much all of them.>

<I'd love to see a picture of you.>

He never replied. He later apologized for the connection on his end dropping because of a thunderstorm and a tornado watch. <Par for the course this time of year and my neck of the woods. Those clouds were headed your way. Let me know if you get this and how you fared. We'll talk soon.>

I later looked up his name because I had no idea if Saul was who he said he was or if he was lots of real and imaginary people mushed together. A few results returned with a similar person living in the states he had mentioned living in. A criminal record for a Saul M. Gentry was from the early 1920s and on a message board for the Gentry-Haals genealogy, but the date was too early for my Saul, unless it was his father. The other results were too open-ended, and the ones seeming legitimate required a payment to view public records. I wasn't going to hand over money for information Saul could tell me.

. . .

Not long after his wife died, Saul mentioned going to a tribute band with his then-girlfriend and her son. It was their third month of dating, and it was his first time to meet her son, who, Saul was thankful for, was in his thirties. <Must admit I had a pretty good time.> They sang along with the Lads from Liverpool, as they were legally allowed to call themselves. For the early years, the band dressed in gray wool suits with black ties and white shirts. Their shoes were highly polished. They had mop haircuts—wigs, Saul was certain, given the tribute Ringo's head-bops behind the drums shifted his hair so much it almost fell off. Between each batch of songs, the stage lights went out, and the group returned as its next reincarnation.

<I prefer the early to the late Beatles. Their guitars jangled and chimed and the lyrics had an innocence.>

<Me too.>

<I wish you had been there sitting next to me. You would have loved it. I know you would have.>

As soon he wrote that, we sat together, sang, held hands, my head on his shoulder, music drifting over us, not because our

OCTOBER

night led us to anything more than what we shared in common but because the common pieces we shared held us closer than our pasts. <I know I would have. I thought about you while you were there. I'm glad you had a good time.>

<And although I love classic rock, I am more of a country guy at heart. Rock entered the 80s with the big hair, neon colors, suggestive images and lost me. What were they thinking? Country was where I could retreat to. It got me through the many deaths I faced. Courtney, my mother from a bad hospital infection, my dad from just being old.>

<That's a lot to go through. I'm glad you had music to heal you.>

<My next marriage was short and too abrupt. All show no go and way too early. I think the tequila made us way spontaneous with important adult decisions. And then I tried dating too many women at once. Not a typo on my end ☺. Plural women.>

<Thank you for clarifying.>

<And here's the thing I still love them all. The good times and the bad times. And no all my exes do not live in Texas. But I go there a lot when they're not there. I-35 or I-20.>

The one encyclopedia volume I had did not cover United States highways. It didn't even cover the United States. But I smiled and glanced at it anyway. <I've never been much beyond Cole and Taylor. Dallas and Houston would be on my list along

with New Orleans. I've always wanted to go to Austin City Limits.>

<Same here for me. I used to ship loads from Ft. Smith to New Orleans all the time.>

<Were you a captain?>

<Only when I was drunk. Do you by chance sing?>

<All the time. In the shower, the car, as much as I can.>

<You should keep at it.>

<I had dreams of becoming a singer, not the lead singer but a backup singer, someone good enough to be with a major act but who didn't have to leave the comfort of the backstage. But it's way too late for me. The Oldies But Goodies crowd would poke fun at me if I made it to the stage.>

<You can get it if you want it but you have to do more than just want it. Life will open more doors if you promise yourself to keep on moving.>

<Ray was a great singer.>

<That's a plus to have in your significant other.>

<He had a beautiful voice. He loved to sing. What about you? Do you sing or do something musical?>

<If I sang you'd confuse me for a pack of dying animals.>

<That's funny.>

<Funny, sad, and true. I tried playing the guitar but I don't have the patience, but I did learn the opening notes to "In My Life.">

OCTOBER

<That's a good one. One of the best.>

<Ever heard "The Dance" by Garth Brooks?>

<Of course.>

There was a long pause before he typed again.

<I always joke country folk ain't so bad. We might be crazy but we ain't dumb. I was City Mouse for the longest time at one point with my work, but I went back to being Country Mouse and now only go into the city when I want to. But I never need to anyway.>

<Ray and I were more like Small Town Mice. We liked the openness of the country and the charm of Cole, and we enjoyed the city but only to visit. We avoided the trip to Taylor as much as possible. When he was younger, he commuted to Taylor for a job he did not like but had to because of money. When he was older, I drove him to one of the big hospitals. Trips to the hospital, doctors, and specialists made both avoiding Taylor and staying put in Cole impossible. One of my happiest memories of him near the end was our trip to our cabin in the mountains.>

<Good trip?>

<Happiest and saddest at the same time.>

<That's what those are. That's why we remember them. You told me Cole is growing because of Taylor and Taylor is growing on its own. You'll have to show these places to me especially all the things you hate about Taylor. Which should happen sooner rather than later because I promise you it will grow too fast too

soon which means you'll hate it even more.> His cursor blinked for several seconds. <Are you happy?>

I turned away from my desk. The air conditioning flicked on. The summer moon glowed brightly. I had not asked myself that question in some time. I walked back after staring out the living room's curtains. My hands hovered over the keyboard. <Getting there. I'm happy spending time with you.>

<Me too. Both of those. Sometimes I like to ask myself Saul do you have what you need? Do you have what you want? Did you get it even though? I think those questions seem like a better place to start finding out who I can continue to be day in day out.>

<I've never thought of it that way.>

<I once read about this baseball player, Corker was his last name, who was anxious after repeating in his head him failing in do or die games. What he thought were do or die games. He placed so much pressure on himself, and in his own eyes, he could not follow through. He went from a hero throughout the season to not adding up to a hill of beans at the end. But his coach and teammates never said anything of the sort. They didn't see him that way. They stood by him. He gained weight which made things worse. Which then gave him an ankle injury. Several fans called him Porker. Some of the crowd held signs so large the television cameras couldn't hide them. PULL THE CORK HE'S DONE. THAT CORK POPPED. CORK OUT $$$ DOWN

OCTOBER

THE DRAIN. I WANT BACON FOR BREAKFAST NOT ON THE FIELD.>

<That's horrible.>

<This sports psychologist told him not to see everything he did as the only moment but see what he did as a series of moments building on each other which he could control once he saw them not as necessary but as a gift to getting where he wanted to get to.>

<Did it help?>

<When he started changing that way he starting seeing his performance as "opportunities" that open with entrances, not closing with exits.>

<That's a good turn-around story. I love baseball. Cole had a minor league team.>

<Cole Cavaliers>

<How do you know that?>

<They played some of the teams out my way. Same league.>

<Did you see any of them?>

<All the time. And when I couldn't I listened to them on the radio.>

<My neighbors Davis and Karen and I like to do that.>

<And then after I moved, I listened to them on the Internet. I get pretty good connection out here in the boonies. Most of the time.>

I typed a question, erased it, retyped it before sending. <Are you seeing anyone now?>

<I had been seeing someone off and on who doesn't make me feel lonely. I did the same for her. It hasn't been much more than that. Not feeling so lonely in the heart and head.>

<That same gal you took to the Beatles tribute band?>

<No. Her son and I didn't end getting along too well. You seeing anyone?>

<It's not time. Neither my heart nor my head can be anywhere else but with Ray right now.>

<I understand. It's tough to move on especially from something like that. Losing a spouse is like standing in the middle of a desert with one tree grown from happiness and sad memories now joined together. Did I tell you about DeeAnne?>

<You have not.>

<I love her but God help me with my one and only child. I talk to her as much as I can. She works for a telecom company after the textile manufacturer closed shop by moving its operations overseas for lower taxes and cheap employees. She is a firecracker.>

<That's good in a way. My kind of gal. Keeps the nonsense away.>

<True and you're right but not all of it. She got two kids from one man and another on the way from James. I can't stand him. James the Stain. He is a "professional dirt biker" at the age

OCTOBER

of thirty-seven. A grown man should not be doing that. Put away childish things. I asked him about it. He calls himself The Stain whenever we talk which thank God is not often. He said The Stain is from all the blood, sweat, and tears he has on his body from all the rides he's done. The media gave it to him. Not his naming but he milks it. The Stain won't do that, The Stain is all about this, The Stain is all about that. Isn't it about time to hang up the helmet and get a real job, buddy boy, man child dating my daughter? Most of his income is sponsors anyway. They're starting to dry up. This guy farts around on a motorcycle and barely brings home enough to pay for dinner. And my baby girl wants to stay with him?>

<He could be doing worse things. Robbing a bank, murder, rape.>

<He was in this promo video for his bike maker. Lots of barely legal girls in bikinis snaking around him. He was out late at night when that thing was being made. Ahem. Not a good thing for Dee to see. The Stain wouldn't do that. That's what he said.>

<No one but James knows what happened that night, and if he's says nothing happened, then we go with that. And DeeAnne's a big girl.>

<Ray ever cheat on you?>

<No.>

<You say that but I can't see your face. Your face may be saying otherwise.>

<Well, I don't know for sure, but I believe he never did because I never heard about it. Someone in Cole would have told me. Even if it happened in Taylor, someone in Cole would have told me.>

<That old saying. If a tree falls in a forest but no one is around to hear it does it make a sound?>

<It does.>

<You say that which says something about you. You have intuition and common sense. We now know that thing has a cause and effect and we've been taught by it and by now we know it will go the same way it has. But not me.>

<You need to be there in person.>

<Yes ma'am. Be there. Touch, feel, smell. Confirm with eyes and ears. If I tell you something you take a chance on believing me right?>

<Yes.>

<Why?>

<I trust you.>

<Even though we're miles away.>

<Yes.>

<You trust me through a machine?>

<Yes.>

<I'm the opposite. I have to see you. I have to be in front of you while you're talking to me. I want to see your face, eyes, body

OCTOBER

gestures. What are you really saying? Doing that strips all that away.>

Headlamps bounded like fireflies outside my curtains. The moon and street lamps reflected runners' vest and shoes, and the shadows covered in bits of light zigged and zagged, dodging in and out of larger immovable shadows, and disappeared down the street and into the summer heat, never breaking pace for the end somewhere deeper in the night. I placed my face closer to the vent, where the last bit of cool air pocketed, thankful Mike had fixed our AC as he promised he would when Davis, Karen, and I could not do it ourselves, although Davis was ready to. But he did help Mike, who winked at me, saying, yes, he needed all the help Davis could muster. And the four of us having Cokes and snacks afterward, sitting in my living room with the cool air on, my computer off, while the forecast offered no relief after sunset, kept pulling me from my distress and reliance on modern comforts. <Do you trust me?>

Saul's reply came real quick. <I believe everything you've told me. We've shared so much at this point I can't believe any of it is make believe. Seems impossible. Too many details. Too many emotions seem real. Not made up for getting something for nothing or taking advantage.>

<I'm too old for that.>

<Yup.>

<I don't think I could do that. I don't have that kind of bone in my body.>

<You say that but there may come a day when that's not true. I've seen people flip in a second over the smallest thing. One minute they are soft and bubbly and the next they are a raging animal you best get out of the way of. It could be anything. Money, love, politics. I think we try so hard to be something we're not we spend all this time trying to keep the Devil out of our lives we should let him in but not let him take over. It's like my dad. He tried day and night not to be a drunk. But he couldn't do it. He had to drink. It was part of him. It was who he was. Right or wrong. When he finally admitted he was an alcoholic everything in his life changed for the better. Someone has to accept what's at the deepest levels where the good and the bad dwell and never has to know why they're there but that they are there. Acceptance breaks it all open.>

A headlamp returned outside the window—one runner had separated from the others, yet this shadow had the same pace, same stride, same scraps of light carried into darkness to reach the others or finish alone. <Someday I would like to reach a better place than where I am today, not because of my behavior but because the place is already inside me waiting to be met.>

<I like that a lot. "The promise of love is to anyone who wants it.">

<Who said that?>

OCTOBER

<I can't remember.>

<Was it John or Paul? Maybe Ringo?>

<LOL no. Definitely not Ringo.>

<Dolly Parton?>

<I have to put it in quotes because it's sure as heck not mine! If you ever want to talk on the phone I would love to hear your voice, Patty.>

<I would love that.>

<Been wondering what you sound like. Like a choir I bet.>

<More like a choir warming up with whiskey and bacon grease to loosen the vocal cords.>

<You and I would be a good duet then. I can provide the tin cup of rusty nails we can use when we run out of whiskey and bacon grease backstage and dry out.>

<That kind of "backstage" sounds like a whole different warmup!>

<I'd like to call you when I can. Been traveling quite a bit. Should have time soon maybe when I get to Shreveport. Northeast of there now.>

<I could use some human touch that way.>

<I was going to say I'll be in "Amarillo by Morning.">

<"Up from San Antone"?> I laughed at his words on my screen.

<Now that would be a bald-faced lie.>

I gave Saul my phone number and left it at that.

Over the summer, so often the voices of all of Cole commented in my head how single I acted for a woman who claimed she was still married and how much she loved her husband. "Girl, you're strong." Gloria said to me one day over coffee, "If you want to do it all over again, you have every right to. You don't have to be alone. You can be with someone. Life is too short to not be happy."

She and Bill had a scare when he was diagnosed with breast cancer. The doctors believed his time at one of the area's biggest military camps had something to do with it. Media from Taylor uncovered chemicals not properly disposed and ending up in the food and water supplies, epically near the Chickataw, but the military, the chemical company, and politicians receiving support from the company denied any such act ever happened—and they had documents to prove it. Some of the civilian men in the towns around the base have been affected. Critics said profits and pride were more important than flesh and blood. A legal team tossed around the possibility of a lawsuit, but that rumor quickly died. Bill's cancer was manageable. The six months he went through surgery, radiation, and recovery tested Gloria, but she and Bill persevered. They talked about her dating or marrying again if things turned worse for Bill. "Fine with me. I want you happy," Bill agreed to at first until Gloria said, "Hell no. You're mine, and I'm yours. Ain't no other woman getting you." He's retired from

OCTOBER

trucking now, and the two of them spoil their grandchildren. They spend every minute of every day with each other. "We'd carry the other one if we had to," she said, Bill nodding and crying with her.

I went to them before I went to Ray's family when his end was in sight. "We are here for you whenever and wherever. We love you," they said. I told my cousins who lived in other states and who had been like sisters and brothers to me when we were growing up. I spoke to their voicemails because none of them were home.

After I avoided telling Ray's family, telling them was the hardest thing I had ever said. I went to his siblings and his cousin Patrice in Skyler. But I should have gone first to Ray's kids before anyone else. R.J. and Tasha should have heard from me, their father's wife, about him before hearing from their aunts and uncles who heard it from me after I told my friends and my family. I often feel I have waited too long to say anything more, to offer anything beyond that moment, to mend that road sunk between us.

When I told Saul about Ray, he didn't respond right away. It was the middle of the day, I was on my way out for an errand at Green Thumb Garden and Landscaping between here and Taylor, and I had to say something. We had been talking at the same time at eight every night, and the nights were shortening as spring came back around. Karen mentioned she would like to see tulips in our garden out front of our apartments. Davis was itching for baseball to start up and watch it with Karen and me at my place. Saul was over the other time zone, one hour ahead, he told me, and he waited for me.

<Ray is not here. And after all these years, I'm still scared and still don't know what I'll do.>

<I know how much it hurts, and it hurts so much. Not having someone like that in your life anymore is enough to make you not want to go anywhere and just sit right where you are and never move an inch again. That pain won't ever go away. It'll stay with you like a scar. I will be here for you. You say the word. I love you, Patty.>

One time I asked Ray if he thought I was cheating on him. I asked him this question from the dining table in my apartment. The hospital bills, the funeral bills, and all the bills for things making life an expensive convenience kept rolling in and brewing up a storm for me. I looked at the computer's clock. He had been dead three years, twenty-nine days, two hours, and forty-seven minutes. I sat by myself in the chair I had at the time—the thread-bare blue one with stacks of papers and folders and sitting next to my irises in our sun room at our old house. My apartment looked as though I had moved in, though I had been there for a while. Davis and Karen's front door creaked open after they returned from walking down the street. They laughed. They said they loved each other, adding their names at the end. They went

OCTOBER

into their half of the house. Their TV crackled and popped for a little bit. And then it was silent, and these facts became my answer to the question I asked my husband's ghost.

When his health declined and he cried for me, I ran—and kept running to him even when he struggled calling my name—and, when I reached him, could barely move what was left of his body. After his cancer returned from our time at the cabin, his voice dwindled into a whisper fighting to emerge from his throat and mouth. I bought him a small bell to ring. This was when we lived in our old house and we had a few other rooms between us, including when I was in the basement doing laundry, repairing something, or wanting time for myself. The bell was small and gold and clanged about like a thing with dents and tarnish. I heard it wherever I was. Ringing it exhausted him.

I found the bell at Farrells Antiques on Maple and 5th, across from the water fountain, Cole's memorial to veterans of domestic and foreign wars, and City Park with its sidewalk wrapping around its edges short enough in distance for Ray to walk with a pace without losing his breath when he was healthier.

The shelf at Farrells had several old bells. Some were so large that in another life they must have been handled with white gloves and pulled from a polished wood case lined with soft fabric. Painted landscapes or flowers circled the cups of some of the porcelain bells for decoration, not practical use. Two bells caught my eye—the same size, no taller than a pistol's handle and as narrow as a small Mason jar. The shapes lengthened and widened at the bottom and tapered at the top like a dress. That same day I also held a list of items the Farrells evaluated, should they be interested when I had to downsize. The bells' handles decided for me.

    Months later, before I moved into the apartment, I dropped off my things for the Farrells to price, and the bell I didn't buy for Ray was there. It still may be there on the shelf—the one without the two angels facing each other and the tips of their wings touching where Ray would have held, calling out when he needed me wherever I was.

    Mom said the reason why mementos and photos mean so much to us is because we have to see those moments again. She had a shoebox stuffed with old photos and once told me to place all my cares in that box as though they were seeds that, when nourished by sunlight day after day, would sprout beautiful flowers. Besides, what is an image but a place and a time no longer around? And how do you get to somewhere you know you want to get back to or you have to go to someday? The images of Ray and Saul take away and give back. Images can't replace what they've captured, but they carry the weight of time and bodies. Sometimes I wonder if memories tell more about the future than they return the past. When they walk with me, they revive much of what I had but also shine a light up ahead in the distance.

OCTOBER

They come back at an unplanned-for time when they have something to say.

Morning light smudges the space where I stand quietly and, opening the curtains, move toward, but to what I'm not sure. Everything Saul has given me I have wrapped my hands around like you wrap your hands around your heart. And yet the month and the rest of the year will go on with and without Saul, with and without his words, and Ray—and Saul—will be with me. Without Saul's photo, the words, and my memories, what more could a month take? But what more could a month give? Better late than never is a motto I didn't embrace when I was younger. Now I have no choice but to wait. To open curtains at the start of the day and close them at the end—everything moves in between.

2

My apartment is one of two apartments on the first floor of a house in an old neighborhood in west-central Cole. I'm in A on the left. Davis and Karen are in B. Our mailboxes, screwed to a wall once holding sconces for candles and hooks for horse reins, divide our front doors. The Weismanns bought the house decades ago when Harold was a young lawyer and his wife Margie managed Cole Unified School District's cafeterias. He practiced law in Cole for fifty years at Lloyd McClendon Weismann. He went to Tri-Valley College and the big state university for law school. He had offers from firms in Taylor, including a county position, but he didn't want to be there. They lived in this house until Harold retired and neither he nor Margie wanted to maintain a large Victorian. They still own the house with all the era's details—columns; wrap-around porch, where Davis and Karen and I often convene; a gabled roof; wood shingles; stonework; and large dormers capping off the second story. Having been re-painted, re-wired, and re-plumbed for two apartments, the house is in good shape. The sun and moon cross over the whole thing, which, in my mind, completes a house and the people inside although you don't always see and hear those

OCTOBER

people you share it with. How could a house be anything but a vessel for all the things that matter, regardless of the floor plan, the time of day, or if lives fill or empty the rooms?

The upstairs is not off-limits, but it's mainly storage. Harold sometimes asks me to get something for him from one of the bedrooms. He does not ask Davis or Karen, though I am sure if he did, they would be able to do what he asks of me, especially Davis who has inquired many times about what's up there and why I go there.

One of the rooms with the big dormers had been an office a long time ago. Harold's desk holds faded photos, yellowing papers, and old ink pens like my Grandma Paris and Grandpa Ho used. In the corner stands a giant safe Davis, when I told him about it, believes has a map leading to a treasure chest filled with money and art Union soldiers confiscated when they marched through the area.

Now in his golden years, Harold does his best to get around. Margie died several years ago. Their daughter Ginny and her husband Mike handle anything we need fixed or updated. They are very sweet to Davis, Karen, and me. If there's an emergency, like when my air conditioning stopped working one summer, Mike, if he can't fix it, will send a repairman right away.

I have known Ginny since she was in grade school and when Ray and I moved into our house several streets over in Holler Heights. That neighborhood was not filled with elaborate

Victorians. Our concrete, asbestos-sided block-shaped house was built for people who worked at factories on the line or in the office but not as management. Those people moved on and left behind homes with good bones and lots of character but needed some upgrades, which Ray and I did until the feet of time and money tripped each other up.

But that house was ours—our first home and the one and only we owned all those years ago. We upgraded what we could afford, focusing on dangerous things, such as the leaky gas line, the outdated electrical, and the broken windows. When Ray saw the termite-infested back porch barely held together, he said, "That is way outside my comfort zone to fix on my own. No way is my big ol' black butt standing on that."

We hated that house when we worked on it, and we loved it when we were done. I was thirty-five. Ray was forty. We didn't travel too much because of Ray's work schedule. Sometimes we joked we loved our house so much we never wanted to leave it. We took little day trips in the car to Taylor to see his family. One of the last departures from that driveway, before I had to sell it, was to the mountains and the cabin.

Ginny and her friends had biked past our house where she had a flat. She saw Ray working in the yard and asked if he had any tools. He first met her at Blue Sky Hospice. Harold's mother was a patient there when Ray was in charge. On one visit Ginny was very frightened and hid behind her parents until Ray knelt

OCTOBER

down and said, "It's OK to look around, and it's OK not to. Your grandma will be taken care of. Everything will be all right. You don't have to be scared here, but it's OK if you are." When she had her flat tire outside our house, Ray offered to fix it but also warned her his patch-it job would only last so long before it wore off. Whenever Ginny handles something at the house for her dad, I tease her she is now the age I was when I met her all those years ago—and she was known as Virginia back then.

 The first floor of the Weismann's house used to be several rooms, where, I reckon, the dining room, the parlor, and the living room once stood. On humid days, the boundaries of these areas appear on the ceiling like fingers running through breath blown on glass. I think the kitchen was in the middle, almost center, where the shared wall falls between my apartment and Davis and Karen's, because it's here my kitchen area starts with its small refrigerator, stove, and sliver of a counter holding a spice rack, a recipe box, my Tupperware inherited from my mother and grandmothers, and my microwave.

 A bar divides the kitchen from the living room. I have three stools Davis and Karen love to sit on—Davis loves to spin—and where I eat if I don't eat in the living room. But I have no room for canning fruits and vegetables. I got my love of canning from my grandmothers on both sides of the family, but given my current space, I make do with few things. After I sold the house, I had a storage shed, but I stopped leasing it to save money when

I wasn't certain about my job. I have utensils, plates, glasses, and coffee mugs but not as many as I did when I had more cabinets at the house with Ray. Karen has asked me if I would show her how to can, but I haven't brought myself to say yes. Maybe this month I will, especially when the temperatures continue dropping, the leaves turn, and we get the house and yard ready for Halloween.

In the house Ray and I owned, I spent Sunday afternoons canning while he relaxed or worked. Music played, and he sang along.

"Know this one?" he asked, walking into our kitchen. He grabbed a peach slice but pretended I didn't see him take it.

"Otis Redding."

"Hey, you good. Not too bad." His smirk exposed the tiny gap in his front teeth and curled his top lip up until the grey hairs in his mustache brightened under the lights.

"I know things."

"That's why I married you. You have excellent taste." He sprinkled cinnamon on another peach slice. "Okra next?" He tapped the Mason jar.

"I'm saving it for dinner tonight."

"Bacon and okra. Fry it all up. Looks like my favorite dessert is on its way." He glanced over my shoulder at the bag of coconut flakes and chocolate bars ready for a cake. His hums deepened.

OCTOBER

He glided back into our living room, flopped on the couch with telephone in hand, made a few calls to work, and scribbled in his planner. His sock toes moved back and forth. He played a few more songs, changed records, and sat at the computer with his to-do list for the week. A piano jangled the opening notes as a few cymbals crashed like ocean waves. Ray smiled into the blue light of the afternoon shining on his face. The saxophone's riff spiraled from the speakers. Fragrances swelled the kitchen. John Coltrane's "My Favorite Things" poured through our house.

I canned until his health changed and my routine had to change with his. The smells of cut strawberries, cucumbers, peaches, and okra still cling to me.

Gloria and Bill and their three sons helped me move to my apartment. Ginny and Mike also helped out. And Davis and Karen helped when the caravan of trucks and my car made it over here. Davis was determined to lift as much as the other men lifted, and he did all his body let him do. He wore a t-shirt he asked Karen to cut the sleeves from.

"Hey, now!" Bill said, smiling. "You got a permit for those guns?"

"Nope. They are dangerous only to those untrained," Davis replied.

The ladies and I set the place just right. Karen and Gloria combined their flowers in a purple vase they gave to me for a housewarming gift and I have since used when it's springtime. I have yet to use it for an autumn arrangement.

Moving here was extra stressful—and not only because of finances or Ray. I have come close to quitting my job at the library, and even if I don't quit of my own free will, they may find a reason to let me go. My depression sometimes debilitates me. My cheeriness with my coworkers and the patrons has dissolved, stabilized, come back, waffled again. As my hours continue reducing, I suspect my position will go away, and if I don't make myself obsolete, someone somewhere will find a way to make me and staff like me obsolete. The library has tested a self-checkout system. My coworker Bobby Montross quit several weeks after last year's round of cuts. "Writing's on the wall," he said to me at his last lunch. I haven't seen him around town since. Some days I imagine I can never retire and I would work—have to—in some capacity for the rest of my life. I don't want to outlive my savings. I don't make a lot of money, the library doesn't ask much of me, and I don't have a lot of other options right now. Besides, I met Ray at the circulation desk.

In the middle of my apartment is the living space. I have a small couch I bought on sale at Fine Furnishings here in Cole—the salesperson told me the color is "cabernet"; a chair I love to read in and Karen prefers to lounge in because its footstool supports her tiny legs and fragile ankles; and at the computer desk, a wicker chair not perfect for typing but is good enough for

OCTOBER

spending time on the Internet. The latter two items I bought from one of the thrift stores that multiplied during the last economic downturn.

I have a sturdy, well-worn oak table I saved from the estate sale after Ray died. It takes up plenty of space in my tiny eat-in area and has lots of dings and dents, scratches, and memories, including new ones. Davis, Karen, and I have talked many times at that table over the years. On the other side of the kitchen and living area is my bedroom with a bathroom. Two people could fit in there at the same time, but the fit would be so tight that knowing the other person's habits awfully well would better than being surprised when the water stopped running and didn't cover up any sights or sounds.

After I said goodbye to Ray, I celebrated a birthday in this apartment. I had just moved in, and all my things were partially unpacked. It was a real mess in here. On this year's birthday I messaged Saul.

<Well shoot HAPPY BIRTHDAY!! What are you doing for it? Anything good? Or are you being good bad?>

<I'm being quiet. It's a milestone birthday.>

<I know a gentleman is not supposed to ask a lady for her age but...>

<Oh, I don't care. I'm past all that. Way out there past the cows that will never come home.>

<LOL>

<I'm sixty-five.>

<Look out now! Retirement! Here she comes buying a sports car, a convertible, blasting only the best music that's ever been in the history of music, buying some land for horses no doubt, working on her memoir that will make her a national star, telling young uns to get off her lawn.>

<None of that's going to happen for a while. I'll probably have to work until I'm in the grave, if the library keeps me.>

<Taxes and death are the only things guaranteed.>

<And getting old.>

<I've lapped you a few times. I'm sixty-seven. Age before beauty right? I prefer being in my golden years. Being young has all the emotions but also has all the naivety tagging along with it. When you're young and dumb you're like a puppy with no clue what to do with your legs or tail and you piss and poop over everything not yours and expect someone to clean up after you.>

<Are you talking about James the Stain, DeeAnne, or some poor kid you ran into today and read them the riot act?>

<HA! No, Dee was pretty good except when she hit puberty. Every little thing, I mean EV-ER-RY-THING was like try-outs for the lead role in a drama play. Her kids though. God help us. The future of our country will be in their hands when we're on our way out.>

<That happens.>

OCTOBER

<I did the best I could. Told her I loved her and these boundaries I set are *because* I love her. She told me years later she's thankful I put my foot down.>

<Wisdom on her end! And a good dad on yours.>

<And yet for myself, after all my decades, I knew who I wanted to be but I sometimes feel I haven't reached that person yet. He's out there. Maybe someday I'll reach him. Calling Saul. Calling the Real Saul.>

I nibbled a few pieces of my birthday cake Davis and Karen had brought me from Fairfield and sipped some whiskey before typing. <I'm by myself tonight. I don't want to celebrate with anyone or be around anyone. I've been this way for a while on this day.>

<I'm so sorry Patty and I understand. I wish I was there to celebrate with you. At the very least make you smile.>

<That would be nice. You do always make me smile. Thank you.>

<What would happen if you moved?>

<I'd be lost I think, more so than what I am some days.>

<Change can be good.>

<In some ways it's all different now. I guess I'm getting used to it. It's still quiet at times, which is nice, but it's different. I guess I still need some adjusting. It's different without Ray even after all this time.>

\<That happens. I remember when I moved from Tulsa to my new place I must have lost about 90% of what I had. It all didn't really matter. It was mostly crap. Who needs it?\>

My wicker chair creaked when I agreed with him and creaked again when I stretched to top off my whiskey and grab another slice of birthday cake from the table. I imagined myself not having the chair or the desk, sitting cross-legged on the floor while chatting with strangers on the Internet, never pushing myself into the thrift store—because that's what widows did when they reached an end and, in the distance, a beginning—and coming across it and the desk as though they had no choice but to speak up from piles of mismatched and used things and call over a widow caught between starting over and staying put.

\<Altogether my apartment is 500 square feet. The place Ray and I had was over a thousand with a basement the size of the house's footprint and stuffed with all our things. We had a shed out back big enough we turned into a woodshop for him and a garage for our car. We had lots of stuff. I downsized here. Not once did I ever consider how much space it takes to live a life.\>

\<We never do. We never see things like that coming and when we do it's too late. But boy what a wakeup call!\>

\<I sold or donated lots of things.\>

\<Did you make some $$$?\>

\<I did.\>

OCTOBER

<That always helps. On the other hand you could have kept all that stuff somewhere like those shows about pack rats. Someone will come along and see the value of some of it and you make a ton of $$$.>

<I can't be a pack rat. I feel sorry for these people. It's hard to let go.>

<Depends what it is. I let go of so much over my divorces. But I will say I kept my dog's water dish. He was my buddy through thick and thin.>

<What was his name?>

<Buddy.>

<That's not too original.>

<I never said I was original.>

<What kind of dog?>

<Heinz 57. Got him at the Bell County shelter. He definitely had some spaniel in him. A little retriever too I believe. Beautiful fair coat, long and curly when it grew out. Summers here were a challenge for him. Gets real hot and humid. We gave him a good haircut. He liked to sit between me and Judy my first ex when we had our lawn chairs out there in the backyard watching the sunset. Turned out he was a Budweiser man like myself. He liked his grilled burgers with American cheese too. And a little homemade vanilla ice cream for dessert. He had whatever he wanted when it was time to say goodbye to him. However somehow Judy got him to bark for the opposing team whenever

the Razorbacks played. That broke my heart and was the beginning of the end for ol' Judes and me. She was a cruel beauty.>

I covered my mouth while laughing. The cake was all gone. The whiskey too. I swept crumbs into a wastebasket Harold said I could have from his office upstairs. I placed it under the corner of my desk closest to scratches from Ray's walking stick Ginny and Mike will have to paint over when I leave and a streak of wallpaper left behind from the Weismanns or someone else who lived here before any of us. <I'm sure her doing that was the reason why you aren't together anymore.>

<Believe me that's not the reason.>

● ● ●

This area of Cole was the place to be back in the day and still is because of its historic homes, but families, moving here with money flowing from Taylor, want the modern cookie-cutters built between here and our big-city sibling to the west. They've built an office park out between the western-most edge of Cole and Baxter, Taylor's eastern-most suburb. A fat square building sticks out over there among the farmlands and forests—tech, I heard, for all the new wave of workers and "economic stimulation" the area has bragged about. And little red flags for zoning have sprouted in some of the surrounding land, like a field of plastic flowers behind Ashbery Street and Cornell Lane running by our

OCTOBER

place. City council has talked about building some mixed-income housing plots, which has brought some homeowners out of the woodwork to express their concern about exactly who might move into these houses, who would own and who would rent, and which tax breaks city, county, and state governments would provide. Most of the new residents, according to the council's studies, would be folks who can't afford housing in Taylor. Driving far for financial reasons would not be a strong motivation for me but would surely take a toll on a body, at least it would mine. A whole lot of time would be spent watching scenery go by—and not of all it the natural beauty of the area.

Our big backyard bumps against a creek dividing the Weismann's property from the house south of it now owned by the Wilsons, transplants from one of Taylor's suburbs. The line of trees spreading along the creek is a place to see birds flit about in spring and summer, dwindle in fall, and disappear in winter. Because of new development back there, most of the trees are gone, but the birds, no longer the number they were, still come.

The feeder the Weismanns put in a long time ago attracts plenty of birds. Davis always notices the wildlife before I do. He's good at that. "Rabbit, Patty!" he'll yell. "Carolina wren over there. That's a robin!" And from a distance, he loves to warn the animals they are too fat and, because of their extra heft, could be an easy meal for the foxes he's seen prowling through the grass and ditches along the streets.

A large blue jay appeared one time when Davis, Karen, and I were out here.

He said to me, "Patty, did you know birds were once dragons?"

"I did not know that." I stared at the jay. It was so big and, perched on the feeder, so close to me I could see the reptilian scales on its legs. "Hard to believe in some ways."

"Dinosaurs," Karen said.

"Same thing."

"No, they're not."

"Yes, they are."

After Davis and Karen argued for a little bit more, I said, "They can be both. I bet so much time has passed it could be both."

They smiled at me and hugged each other as we watched the jay fly away as a silhouette inside the sunset.

Ray's family visited for picnics in the backyard at our old house and, during nice weather, played Wiffleball. My parents were gone by the time we owned that house. Dad lost his job, never could find another one matching who he was. Mother's Day is as bittersweet for me as Father's Day. Mom succumbed to Alzheimer's.

Relationships between Ray's side and me have been quiet for a while. We used to talk nearly every day on the phone until it became only the weekends, a succinct handwritten note, only

OCTOBER

emails, mainly about legal or financial matters—then nothing for a while. I have several drafts of emails to Ray's brother John and sister Carla. I have written I hope to see them again soon and they are getting along fine. But like my letter to Saul, I have yet to send any of those letters to Ray's side. I have yet to sit down and write out my thoughts to Ray's kids. But someday we'll pick up where we left off, and it'll be like all of us walking together again.

    Before Ginny and Mike took over our apartments' maintenance, Harold checked in with us quite a bit, most of it having to do with how we were doing and not always having to do with repairs or issues. He liked hearing from Davis, Karen, and me about our lives and talking to us how Cole was the same as much as it was changing. He was good with email and wrote like he was using a pen and paper. When he retired, streamers and banners decorated the town square and its gazebo—HIP, HIP, HOORAY, HAROLD! Mayor Fontenot gave a warm speech of thanks and service. She talked about Harold's contribution to the local charities he and Margie loved. They were big sports fans and gave time and money to various activities. When the Line Drives needed money to cover travel costs at an all-state softball tournament, Harold and Margie auctioned off her baked goods and provided the girls with funds for fuel, food, and lodging. I bought cookies that day. They were peanut butter sprinkled with chocolate chips. Margie had iced pastel colors on cookies shaped like eggs, rabbits, flowers, and birds. I was on my own, struggling with bills, selling the house, and the next stages in my life. Harold and Margie were among the first in town to offer a place for me and waived rent until things calmed down.

    That day when I bought the cookies I kept to the back of the crowd. The high school band played. They were not always in tune, but I loved hearing them play. Folks knew I was there. I was not invisible. Some of them glanced at me. Some of them smiled. A few hugged me or rubbed my back or shoulder on their way to the front or deeper into the crowd.

    "Hi, Patty, how're you doing?"

    "Ray was a good man. We have many wonderful stories about him."

    "We're so sorry. Let us know if we can do anything."

    That day was a Saturday morning, and today, the curtains brightening a little more, reminds me of that day. It was the first month Ray was gone. He loved that season and loved spending it with his family and me. That day I bought cookies from the Weismanns was very much like today—bright blue sky, some clouds, mild temperature, birds flying around. But it was also not like today because it was spring, not fall.

    • • •

    What I love about the first days of October in Cole seems like they could be the same as they were the day before, in previous months, and will be the same the next day, but when you

OCTOBER

pay attention, each day promises something a little different each time it arrives.

The city folk in Taylor will tell you they know when autumn is coming because of forecasts extending ahead, but the country folk here in Cole will tell you we don't need that. Out here, the sky and the flora and fauna tell you all you need to know and everything you need to prepare for several weeks of colors bursting like fire before falling to the ground frost will cover.

And because it's the first week of October, Davis, Karen, and I will set aside time to decorate the house. We'll organize patches of the front yard for bedsheet ghosts, broomsticks for witches, plastic goblins, and strings of orange and purple lights shaped like bats, skulls, and pumpkins. Harold and Ginny have let us do this for several Halloweens. Mike has offered help, and a couple of times we've taken him up on it with Davis reluctantly agreeing. "We got this, but OK, thanks, Mikey D." Then he and Mike flexed their muscles while we all laughed.

When Harold and Margie lived here, their Christmas lights glowed like an airport runway. The first Thanksgiving after I moved in, Davis, Karen, and I put up as many decorations as all get out. Big, bright strands of multi-colored lights, an inflatable snow globe and snowman out front, plastic elves and Santa with his sleigh and reindeer, and a manger scene. Davis got on the ladder. He was so excited I could not stop him. Karen fretted, as did I. He didn't fall, but Karen, Harold, Ginny, Mike, and I agreed he should focus on smaller projects. I got a kick out of seeing the size of some of those plastic figures for the yard. They were the same size as Davis and Karen. And I was as wide as that plump jolly elf from the North Pole and as rosy cheeked and white haired—and still am. When Ray and I decorated our old house, he would sometimes rattle the ladder as he inched his way up, which became the least anxious thing between us for our time together.

Easter is my second-favorite holiday, and like Davis, Karen, and I do now for Halloween, we keep Easter decorations on the ground. We haul out the plastic eggs and the bunny rabbits Davis and Karen's friend Jonathan Ormon carved by hand. He volunteered at Adult Services where they took his class. He swirled pastel colors on the wood bunnies. They had energy and looked like they could turn alive at any minute and bound from the grass and into the nearby thickets. Karen and I said they wouldn't last long because hawks hovered over there.

"I'd scare them off."

"The hawks or the rabbits?" Karen asked Davis.

"Not the hawks," he said, snickering, which angered Karen.

We also keep Fourth of July pretty simple. Mostly flags and streamers. We have a big banner thanking all the troops past and present. We play John Philip Sousa on repeat, as loud as my computer's speakers can go.

OCTOBER

But for Davis and Karen and me, Halloween is our favorite. Sometimes it seems it's only one. It's our tradition, and something we look forward to all these years we've done it.

And now that October is here, Mike will plant grass seed and fertilizer and, when November rolls around, clean out the gutters stuffed so full it will look like he's pulling out handfuls of fire. If we are home while he rakes the yard, Davis, Karen, and I offer our help, which he never refuses. He always jokes with us about winter—before we know it, he'll be back with a shovel and a big tub of kitty litter to dissolve the ice and snow. We reply we'll be inside sipping hot cocoa and watching holiday movies, so he shouldn't get rid of too much snow in the yards because we would very much like to build snowmen up until spring melts everything, and then Mike will be starting all over with the lawnmower, bags of grass seed, and fertilizer, and the flowers I planted will sprout in the garden wrapping around the front yard. Those reds and yellows are not easily forgotten, and we have to wait to see them. The weather needs to be warmer months from now—leaves returning, grass greening, animals waking from their long sleep in isolation.

The garden at the house started long before my hands knew it. It was there before I showed up, but it was in bad shape. Ginny and Mike said we could plant bulbs. Ginny said yes when I asked about vegetables, but days later, Mike politely turned that down because of the lack of space in the front. He was right—not much space is there for vegetables. My vision for the garden had tomatoes, cucumbers, peppers, and onions. Maybe the way I said *vegetable garden* without specifying the vegetables conjured up for Mike images of pumpkins and squash going to rot, a complex sprinkler system, meddling gophers and rabbits, and his back, hands, and legs out there whenever we needed him to fix something. Ginny apologized for jumping the gun. She later told me her mom and dad would have loved to see their old place colored by flowers in the garden started by their hands.

"We don't make a garden," Ray once said to me. "A garden makes us." Our garden at our old house was one of my great prides. We had to learn from it—its temperament, gives and takes, and rewards after sweat and money. Dirt grayed his beard more so than gray whiskers. He didn't have gardening clothes like mine. Dressed in brown corduroy jeans, an old short-sleeve dress shirt from decades ago, and his thick-rimmed glasses, he looked like a math teacher from the 1970s. We spent several weekends out there in different seasons—not so much in winter—clearing old growth, enticing new growth, planting, pulling, weeding. His back and knees took on the labor until he was very sick, which afterward, he grimaced through.

The small flower garden was in the front, and the larger flowers and vegetables were in the back where our land stretched. On the other side of a shared strip of public land, the Rasheeds built a nice house across from our property. Ray was in the

OCTOBER

hospital, and I was out there fertilizing before the spring rains came. Dr. Rasheed was in her large straw sunhat. On her way to the front door, one bag of groceries slipped from her arms, and a glass jar of jelly shattered on the concrete. I walked over and helped her out. Podiatry was her specialty, but I told her about Ray and his violent coughing and vomiting. She and her husband had returned from California where they helped Amir's mother into a retirement community. "I'm so sorry," she said, wiping her hands on a towel stained like blood.

• • •

The day pours in after I open the curtains. The computer falls asleep. A few trees at their very tip-tops have started turning color. Birds and butterflies flurry around. The screen door next to mine squeaks open and clanks close. Davis, green backpack slung over his back, bolts for the bus stopping a few paces from our sidewalk. I wave. The bus hisses down to lower the first step for Davis. His legs need a little help getting in. But we all know Charlie DeVos really picks him up, not the bus. He has worked as the Route Three driver for nearly forty years. Route Three is a straight shot from one end of Cole, through downtown, and to the east end at what was the parking lot of Lister's Automotive but is now a space of asphalt, big enough for city buses to turn around, with public art flanking the curbs some folks in Cole have yet to embrace. Lots of refurbished trash, bright paint splatters, and metal swirling about, trying to say something, but no one's not exactly sure what, other than the artist wanted us all to know about her degrees and exhibitions and how her art comments on all the world's ills. "But which ills specifically here in Cole?" Delilah Meers asked at a public meeting. The artist had no answer.

The very first day I first greeted Davis on his way to Fairfield he said to me, "I see the sun rise and set every day from my seat on the number three. I'm a king up there. No." His chubby red cheeks twitched. "The king's bodyguard!"

"His knight."

Davis's eyes glistened as he licked his lips. "*All* the Round Table."

Charlie says he's ready to retire. He's been talking to me about that for a while, but the urgency of his words has picked up over the last few months. He reminds us, his gloves gripping the steering wheel, "Ain't nobody tellin' me what to do then. Ain't nobody 'bout nothin'. I got my fishin' pole and bait box all lined up by the front do' now. We gonna fish and fry up anything with some meal that don't glow in the dark when them companies dumped you know what in the Chickataw over there. You ready, Mr. Davis?"

"Yes, sir, Mr. Charlie."

He and Davis high-five before Davis sits down, and the bus hisses back up from the ground.

OCTOBER

If it's a nice morning, such as today, I wave to Davis no matter where I am—leaning back in my chair, if I'm at the computer, fixing my breakfast, or watching the world go by while drinking my coffee on the porch. Several minutes later, his wife Karen appears, waves to me, maybe stops by my place for a brief hello, if there's time, before boarding the next bus to her job at Adult Services.

"Bye, Patty. We love you," her delicate voice says.

"Love you, too. See y'all later." Which has been true for so long.

Davis is the opposite of Karen. He is dark-haired and rosy-cheeked. Her skin is as smooth as a single piece of silk. She is taller than him, but not by much, especially when he returns from work and his hair spikes up on top. He's told me he sweats a lot when he's stocking the frozen aisles and runs his hands through his hair during his breaks to cool him off. He washes his hands after every time he does, like his manager Kevin has told him. Like me, Karen carries most of her weight in her hips and legs, but all of Davis's weight sinks over his belt. He tried growing a beard once, but Karen hated it so much he shaved it. She cut her hair so short a few summers ago, and Davis told me—and her—one night over cards and watching baseball he missed her auburn locks.

After I sold the house and got my apartment, but before I moved in, I started forwarding my mail. One day I was over there, and Davis and Karen knocked on my door and asked if I was Patricia. Davis pointed to the name on envelopes accidentally delivered to their side of the house. Karen looped her arm through his. My old place in town was typed on the paper peeking through the envelope's window.

"Please call me Patty. We'll be neighbors."

They giggled and smiled. "We'll help you move," they said in unison.

"I would love that. I'm going to hold you to it. I'll make us some snacks when we're done."

"You better!" Davis flexed his flabby arms and puffed out his soft chest.

Blushing, Karen tugged his arms to his sides.

"OK, until then, see you soon," I said. "Have a good rest of the weekend."

The day after I moved in, the three of us talked on the shared porch. Davis wore wrist supports for moving boxes at Fairfield. Karen stood behind him with a bin of sugar cookies decorated with squiggles of frosting houses she had made in a class at Adult Services. Cars and the city buses drove by. The locusts were out. And the summer heat was too strong for me. Karen told me their next class was about handling money and washing clothes.

Throwing my thumb toward the back at the house's shared laundry space, I said, "You can use my laundry soap anytime you need to. It has no scent. My skin and nose don't like that stuff."

OCTOBER

"We're the same," they said, giggling. "Thank you, Patty."

Cole is just now starting to have the adequate services needed by them. The city has been trying to get more funds and some grants, but it hasn't been easy. The younger generation helps. I know there are other citizens, family members, and two students in Cole Public Schools with Down syndrome.

Adult Services of Cole County is still so new. It's housed on the ground floor of an all-brick building built in the late 1800s when it was the home of Farmers & Merchants Second Savings and Loans. The first S&L had a reputation of gouging interest rates from its members and burned to the ground one night—arson, but no one was ever caught. The second one survived until Richard Burnett Jr., the youngest son of the founder, transferred it to a bank in Taylor after which it collapsed during the Great Depression. Wendy the director at Adult Services jokes the place is haunted and she would love to find a long-forgotten vault stacked with money that could help pay for a lot more than they have to request every year from the city, county, state, and federal governments.

When I worked at the diner, Wendy walked from her office across Boyer Square, and sitting at one of my tables, introduced herself to me. "I think you have some new neighbors…folks we help out with. Davis and Karen Burkhardt."

"I sure do." I had decaf in one hand, regular in the other.

She scrunched her nose at the decaf.

WILLIAM AUTEN

We had that running joke between us. She would come in around noon, I would look at the clock on the wall, the Mickey Mouse hands moving their way around the dial, and I would raise either the orange-collared or the black-collared pot. Many times, she would point to the orange one. I eventually stopped asking, "Long day halfway through?"

"I met them the other day," I went on. "There was a gentleman with them, but I don't remember his name. They were getting a new bed."

"I bet it was Tom. He helps with the physical stuff. We worked with the Weismanns to find a place for them. I like to check in with everybody. I know they're fine, but it's the mom in me."

Davis and Karen's return home from work has not changed since they moved in. Depending who is available for certain shifts at Fairfield, Davis's schedule can change, but mostly it runs from nine until five in the afternoon. He has slowly and surely worked his way up to full-time. Four months ago, he was Employee of the Month, his second award in the three years he has been there. Friends and staff from Adult Services and I threw a party for him at his and Karen's place. I joked I didn't have to travel far—just walk out my door and over to the other side of the house. It was one of many times Davis was so happy. We had pizza, cake, and ice cream. One of Fairfield's managers talked about Davis's professionalism, productivity, and willingness to help out in other

OCTOBER

areas of the store and how several regular customers have gotten to know him, want him to sack their groceries, and help them to their cars. Karen's hours are the same, but on Wednesdays and Thursdays, she works part-time and handles some administrative duties she says are "boring but have to be done." Charlie will pick up Davis, and Karen's bus, driven by Rose Tuttle, will follow behind. Route One takes her downtown and to the hub of local government offices shored up in mostly old, and some new, buildings.

After the buses drop them off and drive into the setting sun, the three of us greet each other once again.

"Hello, Patty!"

"Why, hello, Davis. How was Fairfield?"

He gives me a thumbs-up and says the number of bags he sacked. Often, after reconsidering, he adjusts the number to higher.

Regardless of the number, I say, "That number is getting up there."

He nods, wipes his boots on the floor mat his parents sent, and shuffles through the front door.

Shortly after, Karen says, "Hi, Patty. How was your day?"

"Same as it was yesterday."

Karen laughs and tells me goodnight.

And before the day is over, as I close the curtains on my end, Davis and Karen get ready for dinner after they greet each other as their voices float through our one shared wall. They finish each other's sentences and out-loud thoughts. They laugh a lot. They love music and drawing pictures. They hold hands whenever they are close to each other. "Kids" I call them because they are so much younger than me. Granted there is a wall of plaster, wood, and paint between us, which isn't fully soundproof, but they are with me no matter where I am—talking, watching a show, or listening to music. We've checked on each other many times. "Good neighbors like the Bible says," they both have said. They've been with me through so many seasons. They fill my heart with joy and the spaces where I live alone.

3

Several thumps, some G-rated curse words, and giggling echo outside my screen door. As I top off my coffee, Davis and Karen move the containers of Halloween decorations onto the front porch. She organizes the decorations by color, shape, and location and, holding a map of previous years' staging, bases her decisions on that, which Davis alters at the last minute because he's grumpy. Earlier this morning he was at Fairfield helping with a late-arriving dairy truck. He was worried he may not make back here in time and Karen and I would finish setting up without him —maybe even rub our results in his face. But his mood changed once he got here and saw we hadn't gotten too far without him and didn't plan on leaving him behind. He keeps talking about jumping out from the bushes and scaring the trick-or-treaters. "This year has to be better than last year. Go big or go home!"

Over the years we've done this, fewer trick-or-treaters have been by our place. They've all grown up and moved on from activities like this, or the supernatural mesmerizes them with movies or haunted attractions along the highway to Taylor. But when they do stop by our place, they start their hike well before sunset. Their parents accompany them, and they take their time weaving in and out of the neighborhoods. Their voices arrive before they stand at our door where we have a pretty good selection of candy we haven't changed in years. And except for adding a few new touches or making some small adjustments over all our Halloweens, we've used the same decorations. Any kind of big change would upset the day and would be too much for me, who would best Davis for the blue ribbon of Least Likely to Change. And at the end of Halloween, I am the frontrunner for Most Likely to Cry When It's Time to Take Down the Decorations.

By mid-morning, Karen stops tacking up cardboard black cats to sip from a cup of apple cider as a breeze cools the patio. I tighten Ray's old sweater around me like I was a guest on a yacht off Savannah. The holes and patches I had sewn when he wore it have not lasted.

"Patty, come here!" Davis yells. "It's time!"

Before walking onto the front porch, I stop cleaning a bowl that will hold a gooey mess of meatballs packed like brains, large pasta noodles for intestines, golf balls with black pupils inked on them, and slightly melted green jelly for good measure.

Fake cobwebs dangle over Davis and Karen's arms and in their hair. They've planted a few tombstones in the yard. My personal favorites are HERE LIES MUDDY H. WUMPUS WHO LIVED AND DIED LIKE THE REST OF US and R.I.P. MISS SALLY SNIFFERS – SHE CAUGHT A BAD COLD

OCTOBER

AND NEVER DID GROW OLD. The inflatable witch riding her broomstick needs the pump buried somewhere in the basement.

"It's time for Stubbs!" Davis's arms pump the air.

We pull Stubbs out of his cardboard box, sit him in the rocking chair on the porch, and adjust his head until his two hollowed-out eye sockets peer out on the road in front of the house. A few cars drive by. Stubbs has never complained about any of the poses we have put him in. Davis stuffs his hands in his khakis after he fixes Stubbs's bowtie, which is black with purple bats flashing big red eyes—an upgrade from the plain black tie we taped around his neck two years ago. We have toyed with the idea of putting a plastic heart where a real one would be underneath his ribs. Before dressing Stubbs in his vest, Karen wipes away cobwebs, dead bugs, and other debris collected after the bones laid under a bedsheet in the basement.

Davis named him Stubbs because the name fits—"stubby and knobby because of his bones"—and we haven't changed it since. I found him at a garage sale after the three of us talked about decorating the place the first Halloween I was here. He dangled on his metal pole in the middle of the driveway. The home belonged to Dr. Matthews who was a long-time chiropractor in Cole, but south Florida's weather and, as he said, "a bevy of beautiful widowed belles" his age lured him to Tampa Bay. He practiced for thirty years in the house once owned by Ms. Yount who ran a tailor and alterations shop before she passed away from uterine cancer. She was only forty-seven, and I remember Mom saying how young that was, but at the time I thought anyone over eighteen was an adult. Mom took me to her to hem my dress for the big seventh-grade dance one winter. Cole had a dusting of snow, and most of the town sped to the gas stations to fill up every canister possible and to the grocery stores, for milk and food, where Dad had one of his busiest nights. But the weather did not deter Mom from wanting me to have some social time. I danced with my circle of girlfriends, a few of whom were brave enough to dance with the boys to songs we all knew and loved. We were stunned when our teachers sang along. We giggled amid streamers, balloons, and papier-mâché snowflakes so much larger than the real snowflakes changing life in Cole for that one night.

I place a bouquet of flowers in Stubbs's right hand and curl his bones around the stems.

"He's waiting for his lady friend," Karen says.

"He needs a box of chocolate."

Davis eyeballs Stubbs. "He used to play basketball."

"How do you know?"

"He's tall."

"Some gals on my high-school basketball team were that tall," I say.

"Not as tall as boys."

OCTOBER

"No, but they were tall for girls."

"Did you play basketball, Patty?"

"No," I chuckle. "I just knew them. I was as average as average gets back then, which suits me fine to this day."

Karen gathers the portable speakers to put near our windows, and I make a mental note to dig up the scary music on my computer.

"We should get a lady skeleton for him."

"Next year."

Stubbs sits as straight in his chair as a skeleton can, holding his bouquet of flowers, waiting in the silence returning after cars drive by. I smile as long as I can until we return to work.

"Would you please help me with this?"

Karen and I lift the coffin near the basement stairs and set it by the giant vampire leaning against the front-porch railing. I place the pipe-cleaner spiders in the windows and, in the corners of the porch, the ghosts shaped from paper grocery bags painted white. This time of year, Davis brings home extra bags from Fairfield.

The end of the month and its scraps of hours move closer, but we have the whole bright, cloudless afternoon in front of us. On my computer desk sits a small calendar. Every month is an image and trivia about famous, sometimes forgotten, and unique sea vessels. Last month was the *USS Missouri* where on its deck in 1945 the Japanese surrendered. This month is a little-known ship from Dublin—the *St. Gregor* that brought some of the first Irish immigrants to this country, which is appropriate because of Samhain, the ancient Celtic festival celebrating the dead roaming Earth on the first day of November. These latter facts I learned about when listening to WCOL. I will flip through the months adding up, after a while, to quarters, and before too long, after three quarters have passed and the fourth started, another Halloween will be here.

By mid-afternoon, we break for lunch. Davis brought home leftover pizza from Fairfield's deli—supreme for him and chicken-pineapple for her. Karen has been trying to get them to eat better, noting the "extra love in his tummy" Davis gives her when they hug as well as the inflammation in his knuckles and ankles Wendy believes would diminish if he changed his diet. But he refuses to eat veggies after hearing from Wendy and Karen a plant-based diet would be healthier for him and would ease his daily movement. "I won't eat tofu. I won't eat what cows eat. Grass," he exclaimed, sticking out his tongue and gagging. He does bring home quite a bit of fried and fatty food from the store, but he gets an employee discount, which helps in the long run with his and Karen's expenses. She always has something green and colorful for them to pair with his chicken tenders, egg rolls, fish sticks, or baked beans with bacon. If my front door or windows are open on a windy day, the aromas drift to my side of the house when Davis returns home from work. Karen tricked

OCTOBER

him one night into eating an almond-flour chocolate cake she bought from Fairfield when he was in the back freezer and never saw her in the store. She told him it was a plain ol' chocolate cake. "He loved it so much he ate most of it," she told me, giggling and covering her mouth.

They offer pizza for lunch, saying they have plenty to share, and I can tell Karen wants me to take some slices so Davis has fewer to eat, but after thanking them and saying no, I head downtown for a bite and coffee—maybe a mocha with whipped-cream and orange-and-black sprinkles. I look around at what will be another Halloween together. When our chores are done and all the decorations in place, we will be ready for another visit by the living and the dead.

• • •

For many of us, Cole is a middle ground between arriving from somewhere and leaving for some other place. Mostly it's nothing more than a place for waiting. Were it not for the town, county, and surrounding region rolling in my blood, I don't know where I'd be. I have been outside of Cole many times, but for me to say I am well-traveled is a half-truth. I know what lies to the north, east, south, west, and most certainly in the valleys leading to the mountains, but Cole always brings me back. I have been to the big cities of Taylor to the west and DeMint to the east and walked along the banks of the Chickataw, which floods every spring and summer if rains are strong. Often, I believe, simply with my own gumption and my two legs, I can get out of here—not necessarily Cole but far away enough from its center and its shadow—and then to where I want to go but can't yet reach. I figure if I ever leave for a long time but come back, I may have to prove who I am and, to those who stayed behind, who I was. Something happens—and will every time—when you're not there. And those who knew you or want to know you again will have plenty of questions.

 I was born in Cole General on the county line where farmland met forest, far enough from the town in case contagions slipped out. An outline of bricks and a plaque on the old building mentions the decades of operation, the overflow of patients and not enough doctors and nurses during various crises, and the brief use at the end of its lifespan as a spa for the mentally stable but physically ailing. Nearby the skeletal building, a new Cole General has been built, but the upgrades have been cosmetic—an up-to-code facility with medical equipment for handling nothing more than the basics of life, accidents, and surprises. Anything beyond that has to be handled an hour west in Taylor, and that drive shortens year by year as developers, businesses, and government officials scratch each other's backs, dividing Cole between those who have faith in past promises, those who trust future but un-guaranteed money, and those who focus on present provisions.

OCTOBER

Old buildings and history are everywhere in Cole, especially downtown. Munson's Grocery is one of the oldest buildings. Ancestors on Dad's side worked there, bringing in produce from the farms. Outside its doors my parents met each other when Dad was twenty and Mom eighteen.

A movie was playing downtown and was very popular because of its story about a woman who inherited financial independence and a man from modest means who, after being the last and least-expected suitor in her life, wins her heart through loyalty and respect and by showing her that love gives those things that are beautiful, good, and true. To see the movie at night cost Dad a few extra hours at the butcher shop, and his coworkers let him know what he should say and how to behave around a lady who was, according to their teasing, out of his league.

"Tell her you take your mother to church every Sunday…and your grandma."

"Your aunts, too, if you have any good ones."

"Not yours, Tippy. We know yours loves the bottle more than Jesus."

"She drinks for Jesus every chance she can."

"Open the doors for her. What's her name?"

"Lee. Mahalia Lee Agee."

"The Agees up by Shaunahee Creek?"

"One and same. She goes by Lee."

"Lee…OK. Let her pick the candies at the front counter. Ask if Ike is working. Marvin, you hear me?"

"I hear you."

"You're messin' with your tie. You'll get hog blood on it, if you don't watch it. Anyway, Ike can get you a couple extra scoops of popcorn when the boss ain't lookin'. Deke and I know him. We go way back."

The moment Mom stepped into the light when Dad picked her up at her parents' place, he said, "You've done something different with your hair."

"I have," she replied, dabbing the back of her hair twisted up like black licorice. She slipped on her white gloves and smoothed her plaid skirt.

"It's so beautiful." He handed her a bouquet.

"Thank you."

Grandpa Ho puffed cigar smoke toward Dad. "I'll be waiting right here."

"Howard, please." Grandma Paris sighed. "You'll be asleep in that recliner faster than a dog wags its tail." She took the flowers from her daughter. "You two have a good time."

They sat in the middle of the row, mixed fresh-buttered popcorn with chocolate candies, and shared one Coke because Dad spent more money on the flowers than he calculated. "They were the most beautiful and biggest bunch of daisies I'd ever seen," Mom confided to me.

OCTOBER

After the movie finished, they strolled up and down Main Street, stopping to glance at shop windows. A pocket watch, with its gold chain looping over the display stand, glistened in the washed-out light of Olde Tyme Clocks, Watches & Repairs. Opened like wings, one side held a clock the size of a small heart. The other side was slightly caved to hold a circular photo, which it did for decades after Mom surprised Dad on his birthday. And when the day came, she removed the photo of herself, yellowing and curling, slid the photo between his hands where they lay across his jacket—the one she told him he "looked dashing in, like a movie star"—and nodded to Reverend Hoon to close the casket. Under a summer sky with blue and sunlight cracking clouds, we lowered Dad into the ground. I have the watch but no longer either parent, and once Ray took the watch to the same shop to find out if it could run again. It did, briefly.

On Saturdays, Ray and I stopped at Donut Spot down from Farrells Antiques for our favorites—cherry-filled and maple bar for him and coconut-frosted and glazed cake for me. Sunday brunch was a thing we often did, especially sitting outside in good weather. But when Ray's health worsened, the Sunday brunches faded away, and the donuts became a joke at first and then contraband I snuck into the hospital. His face would glow, knowing what I had in the sack. I was so concerned the hospital folks would give me the evil eye I eventually asked the counter help at the Donut Spot if he could put my donuts in an unmarked bag. But one day Juan wasn't there, and a high schooler used a marked bag—a cartoon face drawn on a giant donut while cradling smaller donuts—and I didn't notice until a nurse at the front desk said, "They are the best in town."

My grip on the bag relaxed. "Yes, they are."

The nurse winked and returned to her computer, and I went into Ray's room where I no longer had to hide a joyful thing.

Cole's minor-league baseball team lasted over fifty years before going bankrupt in the recent economic downturn. Ray and I saw quite a few games when the Cavaliers were around. I found stacks of old scorecards in the corner of the basement when I sold our house. In his remaining days, his handwriting slipped into scribbles on the cards. Dad and Grandpa Dennis got me hooked on the game and the Double Cs. We listened to WCOL before Dad bought us our first TV. Whenever we were together as a family on a weekend, we all sat around and listened to or watched the action. Before the official season started, the Cavs always played Taylor's team in the annual Battle of the River. The Taylor Red Hawks held the advantage because of more money and better staff and being the last stop for a minor leaguer before reaching the Show. The Cavs never won much except one division title decades ago. Dad and Grandpa Dennis would have loved to see that. Ray said the same about his dad and grandpa. That was a great a year for Cole, but they were quickly eliminated from the playoffs and thereafter never inched much above

OCTOBER

second-to-last. They were the bottom of the professional baseball ladder in more ways than one. Most of the players had other jobs when the season was over, but a few were highly touted and, at a young age, had more money than the state lottery. After the team dissolved, the town lost some of its identity. All the employees lost their jobs—accounting, administration, grounds keeping. Some of the players moved up to the parent club before the Cavs bellied up, but not all of them. Some of them returned to the states and countries they came from—a handful from around here—and some stayed nearby. One player is now the coach at Cole High, and he has done better with those boys than when they had single-digit wins all of my four years. Davis and Karen like to watch the games on my little TV. They talk stats and trivia. We sit in a circle like my family and Ray did.

 The clock tower at the train station is the tallest structure in Cole proper, but a modern all-glass building for the tech company out in Baxter is becoming the biggest building in the county. Several fires—some intentional, some not—damaged but did not topple the clock, and over the years it has been repaired and reinstated to its original glory. I love hearing its deep resonance when I am downtown. An old legend says a veteran soldier, on his last day on Earth, climbed to the top and set a figurine on the lip of the clock face before sliding down and disappearing into the night. Another version says the same veteran was drunk when he climbed to the top, struck a match to see, and dropped it on a pile of dry leaves and twigs the maintenance man did not remove before winter set in. This version mentions, before the tower burst into flames on that fall day, the clock struck sometime between three and four in the morning, after the soldier had placed the figurine of the Grim Reaper on the lip of the clock face.

<What a great bunch of tales! I love that kind of history.> Saul wrote. <It's all about deep roots, the ups and downs of community, and everyone who lives there. Not much changes if you look hard. Some folks in this country forget ANYwhere is not the same as EVERYwhere.>

<I've taken a train from that station. It was a while ago. Ray and I went through the valley and to the mountains west of us. A little cabin up there.>

<Cabin retreats are the best, and trains are a great way to get out.>

<I could take them all the time if I had that much time. Much better than driving or flying, which I have yet to do.>

<Not a flyer?>

<Not yet.>

<You'll have to show me all these spots when I come visit. We can see them from the air. I have my pilot's license and a small prop. You can get your wings!>

<Who says I'm inviting you for a visit?>

OCTOBER

<Who says you're NOT going to?>

<Do you have a date in mind?>

<I'm in Tulsa now. Will be here for a while.>

<What are you doing there?>

<Visiting. Sightseeing. Spring is so beautiful out here. So many azaleas. Reminding myself of all the art deco and the good music. Blood and oil.>

<More like money, greed, and exploitation.>

<That too.>

<How long are you there?>

<Be here for a little bit more then head back home.>

<Where is that? I don't think you've ever told me.>

<Just a head's turn away, by the lake way over yonder tucked in the trees if you look hard enough.>

<Don't surprise me if you swing through Cole at the last minute. I need time to get ready.>

<I promise I won't surprise you, but you never know. Cole sounds like one of my kind of places.>

<Where have you been?>

<All over. Atlanta, Richmond, Nashville, New Orleans, Memphis, Dallas, NYC, LA, Seattle. I have a strong distaste for suburbs except when I'm hungry. I love me some fried food!>

<Ever been to Europe?>

<Amsterdam, Paris, Lisbon, Venice, and most recently to the country in that photo I sent you. You'd love that place. Very old

country. Lots of forests and mountains. One major city and everything else is villages. Gothic churches. War memorials. Legends and myths. Haunting places everywhere you turn. Reminds me how much the present is in the past and the past is in the present. You should get over there when you can. Maybe we can go together.>

    <Where was that photo you sent me taken?>

    <Central Europe.>

His cursor stopped for that night.

I waited in my chair for a few minutes before looking up those European cities on a map in an encyclopedia I got while working at the diner. On top of the bookshelf with the encyclopedia are candles, photos of Ray and me, and inside a bell jar, a lock of Mom's hair and Dad's watch. Somewhere in the entry EUROPE: CENTRAL, along the Adriatic Sea bumping against eastern Italy and the long stretch of forests and mountains, Saul photographed the place he sent to me.

Ray is in Saul's photo but not in central Europe. He's there among the sky, the stones, the people, and the past, present, and future rolled together and weathered away until a single, hard detail remains.

◦ ◦ ◦

I first met Ray when he walked into the downtown library where I ran the circulation desk. He wanted to donate some

OCTOBER

reference materials about elder care, courtesy of his employer, Blue Sky Hospice, to improve our small health section.

"We're all gonna get old," he said as he slid the box across the desk.

He wasn't much taller me, and although I am a little shorter nowadays with a hunched back, I was, and am, average height.

"Raymond Pemberton," he said. "Ray." He had dark eyes and dark curly hair cropped tight. His plaid shirt and slacks were finely pressed. His beard, like his hair, was trimmed and sprinkled here and there with gray. He could have been a doctor, but if he had been, he wouldn't talk like he was smarter than you or had to show off his knowledge and what you didn't know or couldn't comprehend. His voice offered a willingness to be patient with an explanation because he knew you would understand, no matter how long you took.

We enjoyed our dates and each other, and after we married, we enjoyed what we had. We didn't have much money. We lived in our small house and shared one car. We made weekend trips to the many edges of the county and back. We loved our hikes along the Chickataw. We talked about owning a farm. We admitted how much Cole forced people to live together and be neighborly, even if they weren't exactly neighbors, and we also talked about how Taylor, as big as it was, never could have the neighborly feel to it. We enjoyed the little things everyone else seemed to miss or forget because they were chasing big things connected to a certain life Ray and I had in pieces but didn't completely want. We saw what everyone else was missing. We weren't special or separated ourselves from the rest of the town or other people, but we promised each other the possibilities of life independent of money—promises we had to keep when, as Ray always pointed out, life couldn't.

His family didn't start out middle class. They worked their way up and into society. Cole had been segregated for generations, and his family did not live in the white section until laws changed. He said he was angry at what had happened, what was happening, and what should be happening, but oftentimes he only saw violent revenge and destruction, not dialogue or anything productive. His grandfather on his mother's side was a pastor, and Poppa Julian taught him love, perseverance, and forgiveness would and must always prevail. Ray stuck to that as much as he could, but not always. He was arrested a few times for standing up against established rules.

He worked at Blue Sky Hospice for fifteen years. He was one of the head nurses in charge of one of the shifts and its team. He had earned the morning shift, which was most desired because it started at seven in the morning and ended at five in the afternoon. Management gave the second shift to staff members who hadn't worked long enough. Ray was in the middle of his career when he arrived with enough hours in palliative care under his belt. When he started at Taylor's Hillsdale Hospital way back

OCTOBER

when, he worked the late block. They called it the graveyard shift, and they knew what they were saying when they called it that. Ray said to me on one of our first dates, "You have to have a sense of humor. I know it's odd and maybe cruel in the eyes of some, but it keeps you from drowning yourself and others around you." He swirled spaghetti around his fork and later ordered the chocolate cheesecake and two glasses of Port—the first time ever for me. "Besides," he continued, "it keeps your mind on what's really important."

Ray often sat alongside patients at the hospice. Some of them could not speak, and he confided in me it no longer mattered. He didn't say this out of cruelty or lack of compassion. He said it because anyone with a heart would know what each of those patients would have said if they could, because hope was the same. "To sit with them is to sit with life and death, and it's important to be with them no matter what part of that path they are on."

Some of Cole's older generations did not want him touching them when they ended up in Blue Sky. They used the typical epithets. He could not change them, but he could love them and have a power over them—not like puppet strings but a compassion for the sick and the dying who could not let go of a certain past. They realized but did not always accept their dependence on him. Ray reminded me and these patients love is not a hierarchy of feelings. It is an action. Love betters someone beyond who they were the day before.

Knowing all folks in Blue Sky and emphasizing responsibility for them all, Ray claimed he had no favorites and knew better than to use that word, but Ernest Getty ended up being his favorite. Every Wednesday afternoon at three on the dot, Ray set up a small film projector from the library I sometimes helped him with. "Hump Day needs a lil' pump in the you-know-what," he said. They watched old cartoons and movies. They remained good friends until Ernest died.

For all the talking he did about living a spiritually healthy life, he did not live a physically healthy life. He smoked, and tried to stop, but he told me he enjoyed it. He cut out cigarettes but switched to cigars. When I told him that change wasn't good enough, he picked up a pipe.

One day, he came home after lunch and complained about a headache worsening after taking aspirin at work. He had a massive pain in his stomach. He hunched over like someone repeatedly dug knuckles into him every time he moved. His stool ran bloody. He joked about asking Blue Sky to prep a room for him, which was funny at first.

Dr. Corbett at Cole General told us to go to HealthFirst in Taylor. He suspected stomach cancer, but he didn't know how advanced. Before we left, he added, if his suspicion was correct, "Be hopeful, cautious, and aggressive with treatment." That was a

OCTOBER

Tuesday. The traffic to Taylor wasn't bad. Along the way, treetops had started turning colors.

* * *

Protestors marched through Cole in the 1920s. An incident in Taylor sparked the surrounding towns. A white woman accused a black worker of touching her on an elevator. He had been employed as the elevator operator for ten years and never had one complaint against him. She was from a well-to-do family. He didn't call her a liar, but he also said she wasn't telling the truth. Groups formed and armed themselves—black and white folks. Old flags flew and were draped around town, alongside nooses thrown in trees. Vigilantes arrived—all white. Law enforcement moved in—all white. In Cole, Ray's grandparents marched. They were peaceful and wanted the truth revealed about so many things, not only about this accusation. Someone fired a gun in the air. The blacks say a white man did it. The whites say a black man did it. No one was shot, but panic and violence spilled into the streets near Cole's library. The crowds gathered in the lawn outside the windows. Someone threw a rock and broke the glass. Torches ran through shadows. A state highway patrol car drove onto the grass to break up the crowd. Another thrown rock cracked the windshield, which caused the officer to swerve into the corner of the library, breaking the brick wall. No one was hurt. Cole debated starting fresh with a new wall or fixing it cosmetically. Ray's granddad Poppa Julian advocated the symbolism was too powerful to cover up and everyone in Cole and everyone visiting Cole should see it. Taylor had it worse. Fifteen died, hundreds were injured, and parts of the city's blacks-only and whites-only sections burned for weeks. I've seen photos in a book at our library. The ground is charred, and splinters of wood and melted metal choke out grass or flowers. It's rumored that the land where the two sections of the city met was cursed by the chief of the tribe living there and who lost their land to Robert Taylor and his brother Jefferson when they bought it for the equivalent of today's one dollar. The Chickataw has flooded that land, tornadoes have torn it apart, and droughts have dried it so severely any cow or sheep grazing there end up as skeletons. But beautiful flowers reappear every spring, and every bit of that land greens up into fields of emeralds.

In Taylor, a large memorial halved in black and white mentions the tragedy. National news outlets continue talking about it. Websites connected to tourism encourage seeing it. People take their photos in front of it and post them online alongside photos of popular restaurants and the Taylor skyline with its old buildings and new skyscrapers. They ask where the other monuments are—to generals and soldiers, the years leading up to and after secession, nostalgia and the Lost Cause—having heard about them. Outside the damaged corner of Cole's library, a small plaque sits on four posts several yards from the discolored

OCTOBER

bricks bowing out slightly. Only the local newspaper covered the installation. I stood with Ray and his family that Saturday. Poppa Julian sat in a wheelchair, a blanket draped over his legs, and turned up his hearing aids. A Bible in his lap lay open to 1 Corinthians 13:4-8. Henry Younger, a local artist, carved the plaque from an oak pulled from the Chickataw River Preserve. The plaque ties our moment to Taylor's, but it is ours. As a town, we left the pattern of chipped bricks and mortar and filled the space with flowers and the names of people who are now integrated citizens because of what happened. I see them—and Ray—every time I go downtown.

* * *

Many years ago, I could have left Cole. I worked at one of the restaurants downtown when I was single, before my job at the library, before I met Ray or Saul. Early Bird was a diner every town has or had, complete with chrome accents and red stools, mismatched coffee cups, and plenty of comfort food. A man came in one Memorial Day. He was dashing in the way outsiders and strangers can be—trimmed mustache, slicked hair, nice but not flashy clothes.

His dark eyes twinkled after I welcomed him. He nodded at the clock. "Is breakfast still an option?"

"I'll make sure it is."

"Then I would like two eggs sunny-side up, two sausage patties, hash browns, English muffin, and coffee. No room for cream. And orange marmalade for the muffin, please."

I cocked my hip and tapped the pencil's eraser on my lips. "You want anything else?"

Leaning back, he said, "That should hold me for now."

It was close to noon, an hour past the cutoff time for breakfast listed on the menu, but I sweet-talked Jimmy into splitting the tip if he cooked this last one. He grumbled, glanced at the man I waited on, smirked, and cleared a spot on the burner.

American flags stood on the counters and red-white-and-blue THANK YOU banners hung over the windows. Several veterans came in. On their jackets or shirts, they wore pins with their branch. I knew the oldest ones from when I was younger, and I knew the younger ones from school who had returned.

As I topped off the man's mug, he opened his briefcase stuffed with folders of different colors and tabs on the sides.

"Working on a lunch break?"

"Yes, ma'am, I am."

"Must be a big job if you have to do that."

He rifled through the folders, pulled out a red-tabbed one with the year handwritten on it, and thumbed his mustache one side at a time. "Well, it is in the sense I have to keep moving from town to town. I'm on a hot roll."

"How so?"

OCTOBER

"I sell encyclopedias."

The bell on the big counter dividing the kitchen from the front dinged. I checked the ticket. It was mine but for another table. I motioned to Gloria and whispered to her. She took it, grinning at me. I glanced at the contents inside the folder—pamphlets with pictures of bookcases and smiling readers, invoices, and a list of contacts. "I know that one and that one," I said, pointing to a church and some offices downtown.

The man chuckled as he looked up at me. "You working on commission for me now?"

I shrugged and fluttered my eyes. The bell dinged again. "Thank you," I mouthed to Jimmy, who slung his chin up and returned to dipping onion rings in batter.

A few customers sliding past me said, "Bye, Patty. See you tomorrow."

"Well, *Patty*...maybe you can help me." Extending his hand, he said, "Peter Deere. You got a minute?"

I looked around the diner. Gloria sliced Key lime and rhubarb pies to-go for a family sitting in a corner booth. Jimmy disappeared inside steam. "I do."

"Who, in your opinion," he said, loading his fork, "would be more likely to hear about the wonders of the world and want knowledge in the palms of their hands without ever having to leave the comfort of their homes? This man Falk?" Eggs dribbled on his chin as his chapped finger pointed to the column.

"Or this man Routh? They're close to each other here on my sheet, which means they are near each other in town. Looks like this one is a dentist?" Coffee stains ringed Falk's name. "The other...I'm not sure. Something to do with paper."

"Dr. Routh would like to know about this. I can see him having a stack of them in the waiting room. I would go through them when I'm there for an appointment."

"Would you?"

"Did you want your break now, *Patricia*?" Jimmy yelled, leaning through the window. A big grin spread across his greasy face.

Before I left Peter's table, I tapped a line on his printout. "Carol Falk. She owns the stationary and gift store. It's a few doors down from Dr. Routh."

"Stationary and gifts. That could be a good place. People who buy those products would probably like an encyclopedia or two."

"Maybe the whole set."

"Hey!" He underlined SHE in the margin. "Thank you."

After serving two more customers, I kept my eyes on him. Every few seconds he would eat, drink coffee, and click more lead from his pencil. He stayed for nearly two hours. Jimmy pulled me aside and said as long as the man kept buying coffee refills he could stay. "Get him to buy a pie for the holiday. Apple would be perfect. Offer some ice cream. I'll throw it in free of charge." He had ditched his free-refill policy and told Gloria and

OCTOBER

me he would toss out anyone who got on his nerves if they stayed too long.

Peter finished his latest cup of coffee, wiped his face, and started packing up.

I glided over with a fresh pot. "One more for the road? This one's on me."

He looked up and smiled. Orange marmalade had glued a scrap of toast to his front teeth. "I need to get going." He snapped his briefcase shut. "Would you be interested in some encyclopedias?"

"From you, yes, I would."

"It's cheaper to buy the whole set at once and up front than one by one, but we can work around that. Just letting you know."

"I appreciate that." I clicked my fingernail on my front teeth. Peter rubbed his tongue over his and grinned. "Thank you."

The bell dinged. Gloria had several orders in her arms or waiting on the counter. "Patty!" she yelled. The crowd from the downtown parade had streamed in.

"Where's a good place to meet?" he asked, standing up and slipping on his jacket with elbow patches.

"Kudzu House," I said, glancing over my shoulder. I was waiting for Jimmy's hairnet-head to appear and yell my full name again. "Best chicken-fried steak in the Tri-Valley."

"Kudzu House it is. Does six work for you?"

"Five." We closed at three, and I wanted to change out of the uniform Jimmy splurged on because they made us look like "we take our jobs as seriously as a good green-bean casserole" but regretted buying them because a chain restaurant, serving breakfast all day, opened on the interstate between here and Taylor. Customers coming from there said all the employees, from the managers on down, wore white shirts and black ties and looked "so very professional."

"Five it is. See you then." Peter stuck out his hand. His blue shirt brightened like a robin egg in the sunlight.

"I bet you won't even recognize me." For several seconds, I held his warm and calloused hand and breathed in his cologne.

He smiled one more time before leaving.

After work, I showered and changed into my floral-print dress with big shoulder pads. Dress shoes accentuated the white lace. I wore makeup and sprayed my curls in place just right. I was a state-fair beauty queen looking for more than a crown and a congratulations.

I sat at Kudzu House's bar until seven, nursing my drink. The ice cubes melted and watered down the gin and cranberry juice. A few people I knew walked in, ordered, and left. We smiled or waved at each other. No one asked what I was doing there by myself.

The next morning Gloria and I set tables and squeezed oranges. After pouring a cup of coffee, Jimmy added a splash of

OCTOBER

whiskey and stirred it with a spoon green from not being washed in weeks.

"You should get a new spoon," I said. "Your teeth might fall out."

"You don't need teeth to cook."

"We want you lookin' your best," Gloria said.

"Like Tom Selleck."

"I am the face of this establishment."

"We can't run this place without you."

"You got that right."

"We'll have to taxi you to Cole General, but once there, they'll tell you to go to Taylor because you have more than only rotting teeth."

"Some disease from that spoon or whatever festered on the bottom of your mug."

Gloria and I mimicked the scene from *Alien* that ran in town at the movie theater.

"You gals crack me up. That's why I pay y'all so damn well." He made a face at us while making sure we saw him lick the spoon. "That man in here yesterday came back."

"What man?"

"Not you. Hers." Jimmy threw his thumb at me and shuffled into the kitchen. He handed the tube of icing and the sheet of fresh cinnamon rolls to Gloria.

She and I stared at each other. She puffed out her lips, popped her hip to the side, and fluttered her eyelashes until we laughed.

Jimmy returned and tossed next to the cash register a large black leather book with a red band wrapped around the middle and an official-looking crest stamped on the front. "He dropped this off this morning shortly after I got here."

I walked over and opened it. A business card stuck up between the pages.

> I am married and don't want any confusion. I'm sorry if there was any. You should think about the full set once you get through this one. We have a Book A Month payment plan. Flexible. Contact me at your earliest convenience.
>
> Peter Deere

The volume spanned Education through Evolution, and those two words were pressed on the spine in gold. The entry devoted to Europe was near the end of the one encyclopedia in my possession, as was the map, which outlined countries as they were defined back then.

I worked at Early Bird for a little longer. One day after closing the restaurant, I asked to talk to Jimmy and assumed he would take the news badly because we were like family, and it's hard for family to accept change, especially when you bring the change. Sometimes, they never want to see or hear from you

OCTOBER

again. Sometimes, they need a rest between what they grew used to and what they will have to learn to accept.

The night I talked to Jimmy, Gloria was in the bathroom changing into her, as she called it, "date with hubby bubby" attire. Bill was on his way to pick her up.

I walked slowly to Jimmy as he tallied up the day's numbers. The numbers showed a good, strong day, which dampened my palms more. It was April, and the nice weather drew people into the restaurant for Jimmy's Sunday brunches. Gloria, Bill, and I had convinced him to shape waffles into eggs and bunnies and to add extra whipped cream and berries. He surprised us by agreeing right away. Before I reached his desk, his chair squeaked as he rocked back and sighed.

"You're quitting, aren't you?"

"Jimmy…"

"Nope. Don't want to hear it." He smiled and patted the chair next to him.

Bill's truck rolled into the parking lot outside the diner's windows. Gloria sang in the bathroom.

"I can't see myself waitressing forever."

Jimmy waited until I finished dabbing my eyes. "You've always been on time, worked hard, all that. I understand. I really do. You move on…or else." His tone wasn't a threat or a warning but was as though he placed hope in the air for it to be picked up by an invisible hand. His health had been failing, and he had mentioned selling the restaurant, getting someone else to manage or cook while he maintained ownership, or simply retiring. He didn't want the last option, but he couldn't see much of a future for Early Bird. He loved cooking and making food for people, but all those years on his feet and in the kitchen took their tolls. At fifty-seven, he was slower, and arthritis in his left hand curled his fingers so badly in the winter he asked Gloria and me to tape over certain menu items or to tell customers, "Sorry, we're out of that."

He coughed and cleared his throat. "Thank you," his voice squawked.

The bathroom door opened. Gloria knew I planned on resigning that night. She smiled at us while tears smudged her eyeliner. I squeezed her hand, folded my apron, handed Jimmy my check pad, and hugged them goodbye. Jimmy's chair squeaked when he went back to the numbers. Gloria winked at me and doused herself in the bottle of French perfume she bought at a store in Taylor. She smelled like a field of lavender. Bill held the car door open as the sounds of Roy Orbison's "Only the Lonely" fell with the rain.

* * *

Main Street dead-ends once you get past Market because of the 1889 fire when Thayer General Goods burned down and torched everything around it. Ernst Thayer, the middle son with a

OCTOBER

deformed ear and the occasional town drunk, knocked over a lantern near bolts of cloth. He claimed he was sober while he looked for an order. It's around this time of year when the natural light filling inside those old buildings dampen, the hours getting shorter. It must have been nearly pitch black for him in that store. The store went up in flames in seconds. The court and Ernst's family believed his defense. He escaped with a few minor burns, but neither the store nor anything around it was restored to what they had been. The city simply built around the damage, like a cat avoiding water, including the building housing my destination for lunch.

    Far + Away opened over the summer, and I have yet to try it. The new sandwich shop has been the talk of the town—a lot of buzz about its quality and prices. Seems as though everyone I know has something good to say about it. The sandwiches are hand-built with meats, breads, and vegetables from local farms and are served, I keep hearing, with the best sweet tea to come out of this area in a long time.

    Saul told me <I am a sucker for some good sweet tea. Some of the best sweet tea I had was in Opelika Alabama one time a long time ago. I was visiting a friend for the Iron Bowl. Do you know about that?>

    <Who do you think I am?>

    <Pre-game we all sat around drinking the unleaded version with no bourbon and the leaded kind with lots. The leaded

version had so much bourbon you can say you were having some sweet tea in your bourbon. I was one year into AA so I stuck with the unleaded. I was proud of myself that day. Very proud. Very thankful. And very humbled.>

The line at Far + Away grows around the front door and down the block. People I am acquainted with or have seen around town and strangers I don't know at all come in, order, and stand along the walls until their number is called. Folks enjoying their meals take up all the chairs and tables. We say our pleasantries, apologize if we've stepped on toes or blocked a path, discuss the weather and downtown's upcoming Halloween parade, talk about people we know or haven't heard from in a while. Football season has a few more weeks left, and if the Cole High Spartans stay hot, they could make the playoffs for the first time in thirty years, and if that doesn't pan out, the holidays and the basketball season will keep the town occupied long enough until spring blooms. Kids jump up and down, but after waiting for food, they sink against the walls or cling to their parents' legs. A few of them fall asleep in their mom's or dad's arms.

The young lady taking orders empathizes with me after she tells me the wait time and sees the look on my face. "I wish I could change it, but it'll be totally worth it. I promise."

"That's what I hear, and that's what I hope," I reply, moving down the line to pay.

OCTOBER

I have time to kill and debate walking until my order is ready. My old haunts are up and down Main Street and the blocks around this shop, but some of them are gone, and some of them on their way out. Some, like Far + Away, have been refurbished. Dad took me here when it was an ice cream parlor. The brick is the same. The movie theater where my parents and Ray and I went to every Saturday for a matinee shuttered a while ago. There were places we couldn't go to anymore when he was sick or places we talked about going to after he got better.

<I do have a sweet tooth for movies of all kinds.>

<All kinds?> I asked Saul.

<Anything and everything under the sun.>

<You're so egalitarian.>

<Better believe it. I've seen better movies on a poor man's budget than some of those slick Hollywood flicks they pump out like it's the Next Coming of Christ. But some of those big budgets are good too. Those science fiction ones and big action ones. Good summer movies. But my yardstick of a good criteria is if you can sit back have some popcorn and let it ride.>

<Let it take you somewhere.>

<Exactly. You don't have to do any of the work. You shouldn't. You paid for it. That falls on someone else's shoulders.>

<That theater I told you about hadn't changed its inside since the 1930s. You could smell tobacco smoke in the seats, which were red velvet and carved with seashells on the sides. The gold leaf they painted on them was flaking off. And the ceiling was old tin-type with patterns stamped in it.>

<Paradise.>

<Cole is so behind the times that the big movies make it here after they've been released in the bigger markets. It's like a second-run for them, which it really isn't, but costs full price for us.>

<Sounds about right.>

<They're building a huge stadium theater between here and Taylor. Fourteen screens I think. Latest technology.>

<That'll be good for the big summer movies. I used to sit real close up front but now my butt can't take it. Far back for me as possible please. I'm a cranky old man. My neck hurts, my legs go numb. And the sounds are too much for my hearing aid. I don't need another one. Blowing out my eardrum from work was enough for me, thank you very much. But we'll have to see one when I make it there.>

<I would love that.>

But I don't know if my reply reached him because a storm dropped our power in the house that night. The thunder clap was so loud after lightning popped the grid. I went over to Davis and Karen's place with a flashlight and knocked on their door. They were scared—Karen more so than Davis, who, I could tell, was trying to be brave. I offered to help them out and stay with them

OCTOBER

until power came back. The flashlights we each held formed a little circle of fake campfire for us to huddle around.

The couple in front of me picks up their order, I slide down, and another customer fills the spot. Besides, moving around is catching up with me. If a doctor were to ask me to point to the cartoon face on the chart for my perceived scale of pain, and if this had happened months or years ago, my finger would have pointed at the face under the number three—a slight, almost straight mouth on a lime-green face managing unease with a long hot bubble bath and some aspirin mashed into a slice of pecan pie. But if a doctor were to ask me to point to the same scale-of-pain chart today, I would, without batting an eye, land on number six and on the face turning from pale green to orange like some of the trees around town. Moving around too much exhausts me with chasing an image of myself chasing the many tasks I have to get done. And if I don't reach this image, I'll end up broke, homeless, alone in more ways than I already feel, and in one of the assisted-living facilities where some of my friends have reserved or are already at. They say things like, "I'm ready to go, but the good Lord has not finished my home in Heaven just yet." The simple acts of putting one leg in front of the other, bending down, or picking up objects once made me raring to go for new places and people, but driving downtown takes blood and energy from me I need for the rest of the day and all of tomorrow.

WILLIAM AUTEN

    Smoke and sweet and savory smells from Far + Away's kitchen swirl around me. The cooks back there laugh as they move with spice shakers and spatulas. They pace about the room and improv off one another like actors. Flames from the grill pop up when bread, meat, or vegetables flip over. One of the cooks slides a plate onto the stainless-steel shelf and dings a bell. Another man sets down the order on the counter and yells out the ticket number. They are on top of things more than we ever were at the diner. Gloria and Jimmy would love to see this. A woman steps from the crowd, shows her receipt to him, and takes the bag. The bell chimes again. "Order up!" yells a voice from the kitchen. The man behind the counter pulls another plate of food from smoke, which splits like a veil, but instead of the lunch I ordered, scrambled eggs with chopped chives and biscuits and gravy smother the plate. I close my eyes. Far + Away only serves lunch and dinner. They are open from eleven in the morning until eight at night. Breakfast is not on the menu, and yet in front of me, breakfast appears.

    The noises around me dwindle. I lean back, but the wall behind me is no longer the restaurant's brick but smooth wallpaper I touched decades ago. The kitchen across from me, its modern appliances and shelves as well as the cooks who laugh and prep the food, disappears behind the yellow-and-white-striped wallpaper and smoke breaking into strands through which Grandma Paris shuffles in her slippers and nightgown, cradling

OCTOBER

the jar of flour I scooped from with an old tin cup when we ate breakfast with her and Grandpa Ho when I was young. My parents sleep in the bedroom down the hall. Only Grandma Paris and I are in the house. She places her hands on my hands, and guiding me toward the mixing bowl and slabs of butter, her hands are much like mine are becoming—knobbed and hooked from arthritis and with blue veins rising through thin skin. Coffee bubbles in the background. I wrinkle my nose at its bitterness as though I am that child again and would never drink it. Grandma Paris tells me to scoop two cups of flour for the next batch of biscuits that will sponge up the strawberry-rhubarb jam she canned last weekend. She rummages through the pots and pans dangling over her stove. She sharpens a knife and lays it next to a cutting block. Spring rain plops through the kitchen's ceiling. Our feet slide on the slick tile. She throws down a towel here and there. Grandpa Ho has yet to fix the spot on the roof. He walks the gardens, pulling fresh chives, checking on the chickens, and gathering more eggs in the basket draped over his arm, and returns with two milk bottles. Rain falls into the scrambled eggs on the stovetop. "Seems as though we'll have some bits of Heaven in our breakfast this morning," Grandma Paris jokes.

    We set the table. Dad shaves, reads his Bible. Mom washes up in the bathroom. They come down the hall, toward the kitchen, and Grandpa Ho opens the screen door, but before any of them arrive, someone says to me, "Would you like to say grace,

Patricia?" I look from Grandma Paris's kitchen to the back of me where the line at Far + Away has grown and breaks apart like mist.

 I nod yes to saying grace, responding to the voice, not anyone in particular, and turn toward a different kitchen not much smaller than Grandma Paris's but is all wood and iron, no plastic or ceramic, and is crammed with a dining space, family heirlooms, and a large walnut chest topped with lace, portraits of Jesus and Martin Luther King, and a family Bible tattered and faded from the touch of generations of slaves and freemen. Next to the Bible lies a gold-wrapped hymnal that opens after dessert and sits in the middle of our hands as we sing from it, moving through the lyrics of history, praise, pleading, redemption, and hope.

 Eunice and Pearl, Ray's grandmothers, stand near the stove. Their silver heads bob from stove to refrigerator to stove to table. Eunice, Ray's paternal grandmother, is wider and a few inches taller than Granny Pearl, who wears square glasses. Grandmama Eunice pushes up her round glasses tinted with blue lenses. She cradles a big bowl of mashed potatoes in one arm and churns them with a hand missing its ring finger from an accident at the textile factory where she worked for decades. Her wedding ring, resting on her right hand, clanks against the metal bowl. After Ray and I married, she showed me the ring's inscription of Acts 10:34-35. As she stirs cubes of butter into the potatoes, her knees bend and straighten, and she hums like someone listening to live

OCTOBER

musicians. Granny Pearl smells like lilacs, and every time she talks, her voice lifts the kitchen and everyone in it out of its heat and cramped space and onto a smooth path on which no one would be lost for long under a sky so bright and blue no cloud cover could last. On the wood table, I set down a ladle for the gravy and then help place the pickled pig's feet, fried okra, ham, gravy, cornbread, butter, and fresh berries. The table shrinks with all this food and all of Ray's family taking their seats. We cram in, elbows grazing, smiling and laughing as we do, but each of us finds a place to sit and break bread together.

And because someone asks me and because I am their guest here, shortly after Ray proposed marriage to me, I am the first among us to say grace. And after I say it, Poppa Julian, Ray's grandfather, stands from his chair, his broad body hunched over from his bad back, and bellows out a prayer for strength, understanding, and forgiveness each and every day we walk Earth under the eyes of ever-merciful and never-forsaking God. As we eat, all of us stuff our faces and laugh, having come back from Mt. Zion's late-morning service, the summer heat high, the humidity so thick our movements slow in the air, sweat drenching our nice church clothes. Feathers and flowers from the hats the ladies wore and draped on their chairs for lunch fall onto the wood floor. Poppa Julian and Ray's father and uncles loosen their ties and belts and joke how stuffed they are—"Time for a nap." "Salty and sweet and everything b'tween." My hands touch Ray's mother's hands and his grandmother's hands as we pass the plates and bowls from dishpan to rinse water to drain board, patient and noiseless in some ways and full of joyful noise in other ways.

    The sun sets until orange strings across windows and lace curtains. And now Eunice and Pearl, who, before lunch, dragged long ropes of bread through molasses, cinnamon, nutmeg, and icing, pull the cinnamon rolls out of the oven, and this aroma saturates the house, this dessert, this other tradition of Ray's family to have a part of breakfast with chicory coffee and with the many people—each and every one, blood and not blood—who form a family here.

    After dessert, we gather in the living room and start to sing from the hymnal, but Ray is not with us. I can't find him. I look around. He is not here. He is present, but he is not visible. As they sing, no one notices he isn't here. And so, I stand up and walk around the room. No one watches me. I disappear from their lives as quickly as I was with them. I want to reach out and touch each one and tell them I am here and Ray is, too, and although I have to return to where I came from, they will stay with me because they took me in.

    I grab my water glass and stumble into the kitchen, no longer inside Ray's family's house, and Mom stops me in the hallway from my childhood. Mom's hair curls at her neck like a row of letter j's, her hair pitch black in the dim light, her lipstick sparkling red from the living room's fireplace. Her soft face belongs on the

OCTOBER

surface of water on a calm day. Her square heels clack on the floor as she approaches. She embraces herself. Dad stands in the street, his wrists on his hips, his fingers curled toward his back. Leather cap pulled over his ears, scarf cinched, he smokes a cigarette and paces the yard a little way before retracing his steps. A puppy stands by his feet and wiggles his stubby tail when Dad looks down at him. A truck idles before them. The driver shakes hands with Dad and then backs up. The two men wave as the truck chugs up the street and into the bare landscape. Dad picks up the puppy and carries him like a football in his arm. Mom removes her coat and hangs it on the coat tree near the front door. Cold drifts from the wool and her bare arms. The plaid's greens and tans brighten like stained glass. My parents will keep Beeker secret from me until tomorrow, during which they will tell me the man who sold him had no other income except breeding their farm dogs. They were so poor, Mom will tell me, Dad took a portion of out his bonus to pay for some lamb chops for the man and his family to have for Christmas dinner, and then in return, the man offered to hand-deliver a puppy, saying he couldn't take something for nothing.

"I was looking for you, sweetie. Ready?" Mom says to me, handing me an off-white apron with thin straps and a hedge of colorful flowers stitched at the bottom. She bought us matching aprons at Dixon's, one of Cole's downtown shops that sold things looking high-end. She saved up some money to buy them, but when I was younger, I didn't want anything to do with mine. This time I slip it on and follow her into the kitchen where she motions to a small brush sitting in a glass bowl filled with a brown sugar–ketchup sauce. I begin to glaze the meatloaf. Mom lifts a rolling pin and flattens crackers so we can sprinkle them on jiggling layers of red and green Jell-O. She opens a carton of fresh cream and froths it for the tops of the crackers.

"Yummy!" Dad says, hooking some fresh whipped cream onto his finger.

Mom slaps his hand. "Save some for us."

They laugh and kiss. She whispers in his ear. He nods and smiles, and they glance at me.

"Patricia, would you please?" Mom throws her eyes at the mound of green beans waiting to be diced.

Rubbing her shoulders, Dad asks, "Cold?"

She nods yes.

He walks into the living room and stokes the fire. He returns with a red sweater and helps her into it. He sets the table in our little eat-in and strides across the kitchen for our drinks. He takes the glass I had in my hand and, instead of water, tops it off with milk.

"I'll have one, too. What you say, Patty Girl?" He pours a glass of milk for him, drinks it, and tilts up the glass so high, when he's finished, a mustache appears. "I could be like ol' Saint

OCTOBER

Nick." He raises the empty glass. "Think I could make a beard from this?"

Mom and I laugh.

"Save some for Santa," I say.

"Marvin, don't forget the carrots for the reindeer tonight." Mom points the spatula at the fridge.

"It's missing something." Dad's voice fades as he walks to the pantry, opens it, and mixes powdered chocolate into our drinks.

"You'll spoil her dinner and yours."

"It's Christmas Eve."

Dad makes several trips out to the garage with spare blankets, a water dish, and some pieces of meatloaf. He does this believing I don't notice, but Beeker rummages in the garage. He yips when he sees Dad, and Dad's bass voice ascends in pitch when he sees the puppy. After his last trip out there, Dad flips on the radio in the living room. He pours eggnog for Mom and adds a little more brandy to his glass. The holiday songs cover any sounds from tomorrow's surprise waiting in the garage. Next year, my parents will tell me the truth about Santa Claus, although some kids at school have already told me, some of them enjoying my discomfort and disbelief. The wrapping paper sounds like a bird flapping its wings before flying elsewhere.

Up the stairs and to the right, I step into my old bedroom and stop at the foot of my bed. A long time has passed since I stood here. My apartment's kitchen is bigger, but when I was young, my room was spacious enough for what little toys I had—a doll, a few books, and a baseball I threw to Dad who rolled it back to me until I learned how to catch it with my bare hands. Beneath my window, we kept a clothesline before one of Dad's bonuses bought a dryer. One morning a fox crossed from the field behind our house and stood under the clothesline while I stared at him. The shadow of the clothesline sliced his body from shoulders to ribs. A barbed-wire fence divided Mr. Hasher's farmland from the houses in our neighborhood. Decades later, Mr. Hasher sold all of his land to a big-box store. He retired a wealthy man but was never seen again in Cole. I heard his in-home assistant shopped for him and helped him with everyday living because he was too fragile and too depressed to do anything for himself anymore. He was in love with a man from Natahachee up the road, but that man married a woman, and when that man divorced and came back to Cole, Mr. Hasher and the land holding Mr. Hasher disappeared.

That fox looked up at me. I paused in my morning prayer because of the fox's rust-colored figure. Crows cawed on the fence post and then scattered like black smoke breaking up. Barbs burst from the middle of the wire. I had seen other foxes scramble underneath or between the metal teeth. "Mice or birds," Dad explained to us why a fox would cut through there. One afternoon, one didn't make it through, and the mad whippings of his body and his cries brought all of us outside. Dad met Mr.

OCTOBER

Hasher at the fence, and wearing long flannel shirts and thick gloves, they pulled open the barbed wire like a giant mouth and laid the body in the bed of Mr. Hasher's truck.

But that other fox made it—the one standing there in our yard in the morning, when dawn, on its way up, had pushed bands of oranges into the sky as I asked God to bless and watch over us and to guide ours heart in a true direction. That fox stared at me before lowering his head, pulling himself from underneath the thin shadow marking his body, and moving on into parts of the day yet to be brightened.

I move deeper into my bedroom, and standing in the corner across from the bed, and between the window facing the street and the wall dividing the room from the stairwell, the crib, with sheets tucked tightly under the mattress and the teddy bear that was mine when I was a baby, remains empty.

My parents talked about having a second child—or more, if time permitted. They planned on another girl or maybe a boy sleeping, playing, and growing up with me in here. "Big sis Patricia," they said. "Big responsibilities." My parents had picked out a name—either Denise or Dennis after Dad's father. They never repainted the room. Mom cried all day after Aunt Katherine and Uncle Dick took my old crib for Cousin Roger. Then one spring day, my parents bought a second crib, and Dad assembled the pieces upstairs. Excited, I handed the screwdriver and nuts and bolts to Dad as Mom checked in on us. Beeker chewed a few pages of the instructions, but Dad kept going until the dark wood framed a small rectangle on the floor. He cracked open a beer before setting in the mattress. Mom found sheets and blankets in the baby department at Dixon's, and Dad and I helped carry them upstairs. On our way into the bedroom, I accidentally stepped on Beeker's tail. He yelped but returned to shredding the instructions, nipping at our socks and shoes, waiting for one of us to make a lap for him. The edge of my bed was a few steps away. I could reach the crib in three broad jumps, which I tested barefoot when I was up there by myself. Now, the distance would take the two strides I step every day from my couch to my apartment's front door.

After one doctor told Mom she couldn't have any more kids, another doctor told her she could. And by that time, the grocery store furloughed Dad. A string of lean months nearly added up to a year during which Mom was the only breadwinner, working in the mornings for the county assessor and in the afternoons at the armory. Dad got his job back at the meat-and-fish counter but had to quit to help with his brother who needed to be institutionalized in a psychiatric ward until his medications balanced him. The war had burned Uncle Charlie.

My parents left the crib up in my room until I entered sixth grade. Dad dismantled it and took away the furnishings and bedding. I went with him to donate a boxful of baby items to

OCTOBER

Noah's Rainbow in downtown Cole, and Mom and Dad stopped talking about having another child.

I turn in my childhood room because Christmas songs and a large crowd murmur under the floorboards. Once downstairs, I walk into a party hosted by Ray and me. I sit next to his son. Silhouettes move around us.

"What are you interested in at school?"

R.J. shrugs, looks away from me, and sips from a cup of punch resting in his hands like a small glass pulled from a red pool. Acne spots darken his cheekbones. Noise swells, and the crowd's faces, save for Ray's and his children's, blur like light behind curtains.

"What do you mean?" he mumbles, not looking at me.

"Is there something about your school you look forward to?"

He shrugs, stares straight ahead.

Between greeting shadows, Ray glances our way.

"When I was young, I didn't like homework much except for history. I liked my French teacher, but she could tell my accent got in the way too much of proper French."

R.J. fakes a laugh and a smile.

"And she said to me, 'I lived over there for five years, studying, and still couldn't blend in. She laughed with that smoker's cough of hers. 'And that's OK,' she said. 'Being in it is more important than being perfect with it.' I'd like to travel from here to there some day. Maybe those smart engineers can build a big bridge, and I can step onto it from right here where I am."

Some of the silhouettes diffuse when Ray walks through them and toward us.

"Would you like to travel?"

"Science," R.J. blurts out, slowly facing me. "I really like science."

"I like science too, but those calculations throw me for a loop."

A silhouette hunched on a cane stops Ray who stops to listen before reaching us.

"What would you like to do with science?"

"Work for NASA."

"Rockets?"

"Stuff."

Ray and R.J. make eye contact.

"Calculating orbits."

"I can do real basic math but not much beyond that. You can ask your dad about that."

"She's right." Ray winks at me, smiles at his son.

"Being an astronaut doesn't interest you?"

"I don't want to be in the air. I want to be on the ground."

"Not everyone is cut out for that." As I look up, stars and the night sky seep through the roof. "Best to put yourself where you can be seen with those around you."

OCTOBER

"My favorite carol is playing." R.J. stands up. "I want to sing it with my family and friends." The tiny bells on his sweater jingle near the reindeers stitched on the green background.

Tasha only gives me a handshake while mumbling a holiday greeting. Ray moves in to kiss and hug her, but she hinges her torso forward, fortifies the gap between her body and his, and pulls her head so far to the side Ray kisses the cinnamon-soaked air and not her cheek. Stars and the night sky continue breaking apart the roof before dissolving the tops of walls. Ray forces a smile that, when a silhouette stops by to say goodnight, grows with politeness and persistence. The other silhouettes soon follow, and as soon as they leave, the stars multiply overhead.

Ray walks over and offers food or drink to R.J. and Tasha several times, and their responses are the same—saying thank you and looking around the room for an exit, which the room has none although all the transparent walls hold starlight.

"What about you, Tasha? What do you like to do?"

The tall, slim fifteen-year-old looks blankly at me. "I dream of becoming a ballerina, but my mother reminds me how much weight I have to keep off, how much work it will be, how much effort should be spent getting a job to help out at home and with the bills. She says puberty is changing everything about me and where I want to go."

The room, eradicated by the stars, extends into a hall. I follow Tasha and R.J. down that hall and toward a door, where on the other side is the office of the house Ray and I owned. I find the letter from Ray's sister telling him R.J. graduated high school at the top of his class and an honors society for science and math accepted him. He is on his way to college and, with the help of a professor, set up an interview with a laboratory for summer research. He needs money for school and travel, wants new, "more modern" glasses, and mentions trying vodka for first time at a party he never expected to be invited to because the seniors throwing it had more interest in sports and homecoming than in him—but he went because, he tells Aunt Carla, "I guess people change when they start feeling nostalgic even though no one has really left yet."

Tasha, the letter continues, followed her great-grandfather Julian's footsteps and enters the ministry. She is active in the outreach group at her college, reads all the James Baldwin she can get her hands on, volunteers at a homeless shelter on the weekends and holidays, stops playing recreational flag football because of a hand injury, tries veganism for one semester until missing home cooking ("*All* the fried food."), and keeps a young man's interest in her at bay because of the relationship her mother and Ray had. "Do you know anyone who might like to have slightly used ballet slippers?" she asks in the P.S.

I stand up. Sunshine fills the room like the afternoon when windows are fully open, the curtains pulled back. The letter in my hands folds like butterfly wings and flits away like it's on a string

OCTOBER

asking me to follow. I flip the power switch on Ray's computer, but it does not start, yet Saul's photo and the photo of Ray and me at the cabin glow on the screen. I find a pen and paper in the desk and tell R.J. and Tasha their father is sick again, has relapsed, things are looking bad. When they don't answer, the office dissolves into Ray's funeral where R.J. and Tasha briefly stay before moving away from me.

Ray's casket closes, dropping like a stage curtain behind which the gravesite falls into the summer picnic in our backyard at the old house after Ray's first bout with cancer.

"You never see us. You never make time." R.J. clutches the Wiffleball bat.

"I see you and your sister on the times your mom and I agreed on. You know I want to see you and Tasha."

"But you come in here and act like you're trying to be the good guy. You come in here and try to make it all better. I'm glad you're sick, and I hope you get sick again."

"Raymond Junior!" I yell.

"It's all right." Ray palms the air. "Let him have that."

R.J. wipes his nose and eyes. He drops the bat, slumps in a chair, and slides on his headphones while his knees pump up and down.

"I don't wish that on you, but I'm glad it made you realize priorities. It woke you up. I pray every day for you that you walk through this." Tasha turns to her aunts and uncles and, glancing at me, smiles.

Ray hugs me.

The sun sets, the sky darkens, and fireworks stream behind us while many other voices swell and shadows shift.

"Five-five!" a voice yells like behind cotton.

The scenes in front of me echo as they disappear. I blink my eyes several times. I wobble in place.

"Five-five!" the man behind the counter repeats.

After gaining my balance and my sight adjusts, I wave my ticket and step forward into the lights of Far + Away and reach for my bag of food. I head toward the front door and the young lady who took my order.

"I will let you know what I think of this sweet tea. Better be as good as you claim, or you'll be hearing from me."

With a big grin on her face, she says, "Yes, ma'am."

"Patty!"

A hand pats my arm when I unlock my car.

"Ginny! How are you?"

"It's so great to see you down here," she says as we hug.

I hold up my order. "Lunch break from installing the Halloween decorations at the house today."

"How's it going?"

"So far, no one is hurt. And that includes feelings."

"Davis is playing well with others?"

OCTOBER

"He is."

"Caffeine and cheese do the job for me. Better than chocolate. Sometimes."

"Sometimes."

"We'll have to swing by later with the kids for a preview. Mike is over there shopping for Evey. Princess or zookeeper. She's not sure."

"She has a few weeks to decide. She could combine the two."

Across the street, Mike waves at me as Scotty and Eve tug his arms toward a shop with full-moons and pumpkins dangling from the doorway.

"It was great seeing you. Can't wait to see the house. Tell Davis and Karen hi for us. Good luck." Her eyes twinkle over the lip of her coffee cup.

"See you soon."

Davis and Karen blow kisses I pull in. I wave and smile. There is enough sunlight for the rest of the day. My heart is full from the progress we made and have yet to make with the dead scattered in the front yard, spilling onto the porch, and stopping shy of our doors.

4

A flyer stuck in my mail the other day promoted a new church on Belmont Avenue, a few blocks over and down from my apartment. *Cole Daily News* interviewed the young pastor and his wife. He has a PhD in theology from a nearby seminary, and she recently finished an internship for her graduate degree in women's ministry and leadership. They had been in Macon, one of Taylor's suburbs, where they established a young-adult support group at the college there. They heard God's calling and moved to Cole for "the new challenge and simple living." Davis and Karen received the same flyer and said if I went, they might go. But they love their current church. They sit in the same row ever since Ms. Milligan's death freed up the seat she had for decades. They love the holiday celebrations. They have never missed the Blessing of the Animals and would very much like to adopt a dog they could bring one day. A golden Labrador for Karen—or a cat, she sometimes adds, if the cat, she acknowledged, would allow a blessing bestowed upon it. Davis has not changed his preference. "All mixed up for me."

The flyer had a website and a long string of social media listed underneath, which took me aback, not so much because a

OCTOBER

church uses them but because of how long it had been since I'd been to church—and one so close to where I lived.

    Sleek and modern, the new church stands out in Cole like a building for a company Taylor has plenty of. Shiny aluminum and copper wrap most of the outside, save for a long wall of ivy growing on pipes welded into a trellis. Water recycles itself somewhere unseen and trickles from the pipes into a nearby garden. The ivy is so green and tall I'm not sure how it grew so quickly and thickly in the amount of time construction crews have been over here. Maybe they had divine intervention—angels who had more important things to attend to than concrete, rebar, and modern flairs. Machines cleared the land before summer, all the wildflowers and weeds rolled away, and by Fourth of July, fireworks burst from Cole City Park and backlit the skeletons of beams and walls emerging from the ground. I drove by the church in September on my way to get my haircut, and I noticed the amenities and earthen colors painted on the building. Browns there, greens there, a horizontal line of bright orange down the middle. A terrace with tables, umbrellas, and chairs. The massive parking lot had no other vehicles around, but today, a few cars, staff and teachers for the school fill the front half. Underneath the porch leading to the row of glass front doors was a van with HIGHER GROUNDS CHURCH emblazoned on its sides.

    After I open the front door, I wait for a chime. But no sound. No one greets me or steps around the corners. I expect a security officer to roll up to a place like this. The inside is minimal and looks like it has no walls or ceiling when the sunlight hits just right. I should have held my judgment based on what the outside impressed upon me. The entry, branching into halls and deeper into the church, is quiet and peaceful. I am here unannounced.

In the sanctuary, a cross hangs over the stage, where, in my childhood church and in Ray's, a choir stood behind the clergy. But this stage has a drum kit, guitar stands and amplifiers, and a keyboard long enough for a touring band. Behind that equipment dangles a large video screen. Rows of colored lights hover over me. I rub my hands over fabric on the front and back padding the seats. Sitting here would not be hard on a body while waiting for the sermon and singing to begin or end.

Last time I stood in a church, Ray's body lay in an open casket at the front where, for the memorial service, Reverend Bowman, a short, stout man with white hair wrapping the bottom half of his head, eulogized the life of my husband, a father, a brother, a son and grandson, a nephew, an uncle, and "a citizen of our local community who served his days through Christ." We cried and laughed and were quiet and loud all day long and for days afterward.

Mt. Zion was Ray's church when he was growing up and after he left Taylor. Before condos, restaurants, and shopping districts for a different and growing demographic sprung around it, its narrow steeple could be seen striking through the leaves of

OCTOBER

surrounding trees like a gray iron string pulled tightly into the blue sky and capped off with a cross, according to oral tradition, inscribed with the Biblical verse SING AND MAKE MELODY IN YOUR HEART TO THE LORD – A.D. MAY 5 1889. When Ray's great aunt, leaning on her walker and wearing a pink dress and pillbox hat, told me about it my first time there, I looked up, squinted at sunlight, and couldn't confirm it with my eyes, but I believed her.

As courting lovebirds, as newlyweds, as an old married couple, we attended services whenever we visited his family. Freemen and descendants of slaves built the church with materials they scavenged from towns, farms, and the things they brought with them and from the nearby forests, harvesting poplar and, for the strongest support, the big oaks whose trunks, branches, and roots soaked up rains and water flowing under the land near the Chickataw. Some of the men knew blacksmithing and converted horseshoes, harnesses, and rusted pails into nails, coat and hat hooks, and metalwork. The floors creaked, the walls buckled, especially during thunderstorms, and the summer heat and humidity drenched the faces and bodies of everyone sitting or standing in that tiny sanctuary. Their voices sang and spoke through moisture thick in the air that could not weigh down the echoes under the rafters and roof.

Air conditioning and heating didn't arrive anytime soon, which is still a running joke with the current congregation—"Hot as Hell but as welcoming as Heaven." In the 1970s, steel beams reinforced the original wood of the sanctuary and the alcove. A concrete foundation replaced the century-old dirt and straw. Over the decades, new paint was applied over layers of the old paint that wasn't, or couldn't be, scraped off. The portrait of Dr. Martin Luther King hangs over at least three different colors on the east wall.

    Taylor designated Mt. Zion an historic landmark shortly after its one-hundredth birthday, a status made possible by Ray and his family. We were all so proud that day, so full of life and hope. Electric lights were installed over the pews and on the sides of the entrance door, which, as Reverend Johnson liked to remind us in a parable, not simply a story with facts, had seen its share of boots marking and kicking it; fists pounding on it; anger, threats, and confusion churning; and finally love waiting outside. She told this parable while she held the old knobs and locks in her hands, telling us the key to entering was, is, and always will be inside the hearts and minds of people who want to hear the Good News accessible to anyone who asks for it.

    My childhood church was roughly the same size of Mt. Zion —and in the same shape, given its old foundation, roof, and walls —but nowhere near the size of Higher Grounds. First Avenue was one of the few Methodist churches in the middle of a county dominated by Baptists and Pentecostals. The Episcopalians had a stronghold in the cities, and the Catholics were sprinkled

OCTOBER

throughout the towns and the countryside. A mixed congregation had gone to First Methodist for a long time. Most of us did not come from the upper class. Some of us kids went to college, but most followed in the footsteps of hired hands, farmers, and small-business owners who lived and died in the same area as generations before them. Some of the boys I knew joined the military—by choice or by draft. And some of us there weren't Methodist at all. They were becoming or thinking about it or there for the time being, for reasons they shared or didn't share. But Pastor Cheek would not let any of us walk away without an engaging talk and good food and drink. He took us all in, judged no one, and asked we see who he was, representing the church, whom he served, and how the Body of Christ could transform us, if we asked and received. All of us deserved love and a new life, but we had to answer a call greater than ourselves.

<I once was lost too.> Saul wrote.

<And now?>

<I wouldn't say I've earned my wings, but I'm doing the best I can with it all. Pretty typical path. Being taught one way of thinking, rebelling, doubting, then accepting little by little.>

<Where are you with that?>

<Moving from one to the other. Sometimes somedays right in the middle. Somedays it's a bit of a backslide but not too far back into that one end. I get back up and move toward the better end.>

Faith carried Ray when his body no longer could, when pain overwhelmed him. No chemical cocktail prescribed by the oncologists strengthened or moved him the same way. Chemotherapy erased his hair—and did again, in waves, when new hair returned and when he relapsed. He struggled scrubbing his back. I helped him in the shower where he moved like a ghost passing through light and water behind glass. Loss of appetite dwindled him to half his weight. He was so skinny he could have slipped through the gap in the basement door he never fixed, where the cold winter or hot summer wind seeped through. We laughed about it, but the joke didn't last very long before we quieted. One leg dragged before his other leg could catch up. Daily his body broke down, until it let go of him.

But he also let go of his body because of his faith. Ray didn't want to return to the life he had. He couldn't stop the inevitable, but he could step into it free of any earthly weight. Through all his highs and lows, especially during his final days, he never abandoned his belief in something benevolent, unseen, and present. Nothing material could reduce his trust in spiritual matter. Even as doctors and his medications reached their limits and could only, as Dr. Randisky said to us after Ray vomited blood, "control what's there but can't stop anything new," he remained the same. He was never nervous or scared. The more cancer took from him, the more his faith gave back, driving him forward even when I assumed we had moved backward. Faith

OCTOBER

filled him so much and spilled out whenever he broke open, and it touched everyone who knew him. He sang more. Near the end, hallucinations came on frequently. He spoke with family and friends—dead and alive—and as he talked, his hands drew maps in the air.

In the hallway between our bedroom and the bathroom at the old house, I found him curled on the rug with the long scratchy fibers he complained about after we bought it. His feet could not walk across it without socks. I promised to buy him slippers with rubber soles for his next birthday. He was barely conscious. I scooped him up, placed him in the passenger's seat, and drove us to HealthFirst in Taylor. The radio buzzed while we sat in traffic. I adjusted the knob. A song we loved came on. The engine idled. "When I pulled everything from the flames, you were there waiting as you said you would," the singer sang over guitar and drums.

When the song's last note ended, Ray wiped his face and switched to the sports station. Taylor University had a home game against Newman State, and when the Golden Knights reached a first down against the Cardinals, a siren screamed. It was a decades-old tradition for TU. Before modern electricity, the students elected a senior to call out first downs through a large golden megaphone shaped like a ram's horn. Ray liked to roll the game's program, hold it to his lips like a trumpet, and shout along with the siren—along with everyone else in the stands. An alum found an old tornado siren, cleaned it up, and donated it to the athletics department, which installed it over the main press box at the stadium and was so loud Ray's grandparents heard it from where they lived several neighborhoods away in what had been the blacks-only part of town.

We waited in the same hospital room—Ray on the bed with devices plugged into him; me in the chair pulled alongside—where we began when his symptoms first appeared seemed so long ago yet too soon to return. Ending at the start was not lost on Ray. He twisted his head at me and mumbled this observation through his oxygen mask. The sound cut through like light in fog. I knew right away what he said.

Long before he became sick, he said faith was not about control but was about following wherever it led—"an act of following," he said. Faith may hide or shrink into a shadow cast by a large doubt with broad wings, a pointed tail, and fangs, but it would emerge at the right time and place. It was everywhere, always, and forever. Ray knew, in the present, he wouldn't be healed, but he also knew, in the future, he would be whole. Many years passed, leading to his final hospital stay, until Ray reached that point—to know we are exactly where we are meant to be before we had to be somewhere else.

· · ·

OCTOBER

My grandmother's death was the first time I struggled hearing faith pull me back to it or call me further on up ahead. I sat in the row closest to the windows and in the third-to-last seat in Miss Willingham's science class. Cole Junior High reeked of cafeteria food stored in lockers, dares and pranks lingering in the boys' bathrooms, experiments gone wrong in science labs and home economics, and smells unwashed from the gym. The wall where a baseball player launched a fastball during winter practice had been patched but stood out with its mismatched paint.

Brady Thomas sat in front of me. His red hair glowed less like fire and more like autumn leaves, but the day my grandmother died was in February when his older brother's checkered jacket draped off his shoulders and dangled below his chubby, calloused hands. The window next to him, because of a large crack running from pane to pane, could not close all the way. Chelsea O'Halloran sat behind me. She wore pigtails nearly every day, and with her hair pulled from her face, her freckles and small button-nose were prominent. We knew everyone around us. We had lived in the same areas and had gone to school functions and community events since we were young. A few new faces arrived over the years from other parts of the county, the state, or out of state or returned back home, like Coach Gibson who moved from Cantrell in order for his wife to take care of her father Donald Childress, whom we all knew because he gave tours on his farm with a clunky, rusted tractor and hay trailer. But mostly we were familiar with each other. Everyone was within some kind of distance.

Miss Willingham was a portly woman with square glasses and a headful of thick curly short hair. She wore dresses printed with pastel flowers—and never wore another style. My classmates often snickered not because she sewed her dresses but because she sewed them without the accuracy and perfection of my classmates' mothers, sisters, aunts, great aunts, and grandmothers. I didn't care for them teasing Miss Willingham behind her back, but at times I giggled at the sight of a frayed hemline big enough for fish to swim through. The freshmen who had been in her class the previous year told us she assigned plenty of homework, which often required outside-of-class activities or hands-on experiments to understand concepts, and she was a stickler for written reports, especially for us communicating as best we could and in our own voices what we experienced. And as opposed to other teachers, such as Mr. Reed's nose-picking while grading papers, those were their only complaints about her. Scientific concepts very much interested me, but I was an average science student. Miss Willingham was intelligent and articulate, and I never forgot the Periodic Table lowering from the ceiling as she told us everything in life had a structure of elements sometimes seen, sometimes hidden, but always present.

This one day she was in the middle of writing on the chalkboard. Her cursive writing could be read from any spot in

OCTOBER

the room, and she cleaned the blackboard every morning before we took our seats until it shined like a freshly brushed horse. She finished writing NEWTON'S FIRST LAW and started to explain it when the door opened.

Principal Van Dorn usually knocked, but this time he walked in without a greeting, acknowledged her, and scanned our faces. "Patricia Maddux," he said, the t's and d's of spoken hard.

Desks and chairs squeaked, and all the kids' eyes landed on me. I assumed the worst but could not think what I had done. I had argued with Carrie Anne Reeves about isolation and community in *The Hunchback of Notre Dame* in English class, but Mrs. Holmes appreciated our spunk and did not reprimand us.

Miss Willingham nodded and smiled at me.

I stood up and started forward when he stopped me.

"Bring your things."

Down the hallway we walked. Sunlight brightened the windows and silhouetted the bare trees. Some classroom doors were open, and my peers gawked at me while I walked with the principal, which is what I had done too. If someone walked by with the nurse, we were jealous because, whether you were really sick or put on a good-enough performance to be seen as sick and dismissed, someone was headed home early.

"No, this way," he said when I turned for the main office.

My parents' car idled in the parking lot. Dad waited beside it. His coat collar was pulled around his neck. His hair was waxed back on the sides, but the wind picked it up. He was still dressed for work in his shirt, tie, slacks, and nice shoes. Four months had passed since he became assistant manager of the meat and seafood department at Fairfield. We were so proud of him, and it was a nice Christmas present that year. He didn't have to wear his butcher's smock as much because his new role placed him in charge of deliveries, bank runs, and handling accounts. He had to look more business-like, which he admitted would take some time getting used to. When Principal Van Dorn and I emerged, Dad stamped out his cigarette and smiled at me. The two men shook hands. Dad set my belongings in the trunk, except for my lunch, alongside tire chains, a bag of melting salt, a pick axe, blankets, lanterns, and a box of candy bars. He said we would be driving straight through, no stopping, and I should eat now. He always complained about our car starting again and braking under poor driving conditions. He offered a canteen of water. Mom sat in the passenger seat and didn't acknowledge me.

"Probably back Monday," Dad said.

Principal Van Dorn nodded, waved to me, and headed inside.

My peers stared from the classroom windows. Brady Thomas looked like a giant checkerboard. Miss Willingham returned to the blackboard and drew a line from ACTION to OUTSIDE FORCE.

OCTOBER

Dad put the car in gear and pulled out of the parking lot.

"Where are we going?" I asked, placing a handful of potato chips in my napkin on my lap.

Mom turned around, lowered her sunglasses. Her eyes were red. Mascara ran down her cheeks. "Patty." She touched my knee. "Grandma Paris has died."

"What?"

"I'm so sorry, sweetie."

I mumbled "No," and it echoed as I pressed my head against the window and cried into the glass holding my breath and growing colder as we headed out of town.

"We know you loved her as much as we did."

I nicknamed Mom's mom Grandma Paris. One of her bookshelves at her old house had a black-and-white photo of her as a young woman standing at the base of the Eiffel Tower. Verlene, her friend and coworker, snapped it. As soon as they graduated high school, she and Verlene took a train to Miami, Florida, worked as housekeeping on an ocean liner, and crossed the Atlantic—her only way of getting out of where she had been her whole life. Outside a café near the Seine, she met Grandpa Ho who had stayed in France after the war. They drank, ate dinner, and talked all night. He planned on taking his time getting back to the States and buying a snazzy but badly damaged Italian sports car he could refurbish after shipping it, but for the same price, he could rent a room and, for several times more than the cost of the car, ride the same boat she rode. "Howard Agee," he said as he kissed her hand after she offered it and said, "Marigold Mabel Reuters."

"How did she die?"

Mom started to speak but stopped herself with a handkerchief. Dad reached for her while turning down a single-lane country road.

"There was an accident," he answered me. "She was on her way to the store when a car jumped the curb."

Sniffling, Mom traded her handkerchief for knitting supplies. "Eat up, sweetie. We can't stop until we get there."

The first chip had no flavor, the second made me sick, and not enough water washed away the salt from them or my cheeks. Dad caught up to several of the cars and trucks that had flown past us on the highway, but it didn't feel like he was speeding. It felt like I was in a box, and everything alive outside that box moved in many directions while I sat still with the illusion of moving in one direction. I wiped sweat with my napkin but chilled immediately. I yawned but wasn't tired. I ached but had not left the back seat. I closed my eyes, but nothing stopped smothering me. I set aside the chips and canteen and wished for something other than food and water and the car quickening to an end somewhere in the darkness.

"How old was she?"

"Seventy-two. A strong, stubborn seventy-two."

OCTOBER

"That she was," Dad agreed with Mom. "Tragic accident."

Up to that point in my life, I had never lost anyone close to me. Farming and farmers in the family shaped my understanding of death and the distance from it to me. I helped my aunt string chickens on the clothesline in her backyard before she went down the row with a knife in her hand, which bothered my cousins, but for me, it was uncomfortable but not sad. I never asked questions about death, and no one told me about it or asked me if I had questions. I knew it was an absence, like when a character I had seen in a movie or read in a book disappeared, and the effects and causes were sometimes seen—movement strung between the two. But even if it wasn't seen or talked about, it was with us, like sounds, wrapped neither tight nor loose and attached to God, Heaven, and all things living on Earth.

"We brought some books from your room." Mom turned to me with a stack after finishing a row of yarn the color of a clear spring sky.

"There's a flashlight behind me," Dad said, looking at me from the rearview mirror.

As we drove north of Cole, the terrain changed from hills, rolling acres, and forests into foothills and hamlets tucked in nooks. Billboards for restaurants, shops, and attractions rushed by. Wintry browns and grays closed in around the Tri-Valley. Mountains grew on the horizon. The sun and temperature dropped some more. The apple and peach orchards I had played in and picked from on our trips through here spread like wires through the sky. I knew where we were headed.

"This isn't mine." I held up the book.

Dad glanced at Mom who didn't stop knitting.

"It's yours, sweetie," she said.

After the car skidded a bit, Dad pulled to the roadside and rummaged in the trunk. Chains clanked on the ground before slapping the tires.

"You should read it," Mom said.

"Did it come from the library?"

"We'll be there soon."

Dad opened my door and wrapped my legs in a blanket. "Find that flashlight?" He kissed my forehead, handed the other blanket to Mom, and got the car going after he cursed its sputtering and coughing.

I clicked on the flashlight and trembled at the title. I didn't want to go past the cover with the little boy wondering why his grandfather no longer fished alongside him. He looked sad standing alone by the pond, holding his pole and tackle box, waiting for the space to fill between water and grass. Wind, tires crunching, Mom's needles, and my breathing and sniffling were the only sounds until I finished the book, and then the words and pictures were the only sounds I heard although we reached Uncle Dick and Aunt Katherine's house where Mom's family waited with all their noise. I left the book on the back seat, but it

OCTOBER

followed me into the guest room; to the big warm meal prepared for all of us; into family memories; into the rest of the night and my dreams of hearing but never finding Grandma Paris play an organ in a field staked with pieces of cloth billowing like flags; and into morning and a line of people at church waiting to touch and speak to Grandma Paris one last time. And when it was our turn, I held Mom's hand, Dad behind us, his hands on our shoulders, and we stood at the casket.

"Mrs. Kimble and her sisters prepared her with great care and attention, washing and dressing her," Mom said, nodding at Grandma Paris's mass of silver curls. "Greta did a great job on her hair."

"She sure did." Dad dabbed his eyes with his tie.

"And I know they talked to her the whole time, chatting away and catching her up on all the latest." Mom laid her sky-colored knitting in the casket after Dad added a photo of Grandma Paris and Grandpa Ho picnicking in the Blue Ridge Mountains. "Do you remember something about her? Something she can take with her?"

I moved closer to Grandma Paris laying in her purple-and-blue dress with lace on the collar and sleeves. Down at her stockings, her shoes were pearls. Makeup and lipstick brightened her face. Her hands rested in her lap, wedding ring on her finger, as though, like the book described, her body fell asleep, her soul reunited in Heaven with God and everyone she knew and loved who went before her. The narrator said feeling pain and joy at the same time was normal as was wondering why God would allow such a thing to people we never want to let go. "She always talked for a long time before losing her breath."

"She *loved* to talk."

"Grandpa Ho could get going with her," Dad said. "And then Zip would join in and bark his head off."

"She told me poems and quotes." My lips quivered. "She mumbled some of the words but good enough. She told me French things."

"None of us would be here without her going there, and the two of them meeting."

"You didn't marry up, but you and Dad made each other rich," Mom whispered to the casket, chuckling with Dad.

"I know she prayed and read the Bible every day. People tell me I look like her."

"You do," my parents said.

"I want to be like her when I get older." Touching Grandma Paris's hand was like touching a cold, hard surface. I wondered if my classmate were studying the same thing when I left, standing at the blackboard at the front of the room in winter light and among skeletal trees outside windows, and following through on a series Miss Willingham, before drifting to the back of the room, placed before them to solve—like heavy objects arriving like

OCTOBER

surprises—which would remain incomplete until they approached with their ghostly chalk marks. "She's not asleep," I mumbled.

My parents looked at me.

"The book said she'd be asleep like the boy's grandfather, but she's not." I gripped the casket lining. "She's not asleep or awake. She's gone, and God shouldn't have taken her. God shouldn't have jumped that car onto her." I turned around. "And if she's in Heaven, what's here? What are we giving all this to?"

The cemetery was a few miles down from the church. My parents had joked, back in the days when families and folks moved further from their church, it became less convenient to die because either the church had to come for you, which cost them time and money, or someone who knew you brought your body to the church, which cost that person time and money. That was why, my parents said, old cemeteries were a luxury and a good partner for life. "You didn't have to go anywhere else," Dad said. "You had a place waiting to take you in."

Before we left the burial, Mom and I walked among a good number of our family's tombstones carved with names, dates, relationships, and sometimes a quote, which was often religious. On the graves we placed some flowers from the service and stood quietly in our black dresses. Mom's hand was warm. She said she wanted her stone to quote Matthew 6:34—Don't worry about tomorrow. All Dad cared about, when his time came, resting in eternity next to her. I had wanted Psalm 23:4 inscribed on my stone because it was a favorite of my grandparents, especially Grandpa Ho who said he scratched it on the inside of his helmet during the war, but standing at Grandma Paris's grave, only the dark valley, shadows, and bitter wind were with me. I wanted a stone with only my name and dates or no stone at all sitting still but not alone in the middle of grass, trees, and the weather. "L'ombre," Grandma Paris said to me one summer day after baking cookies and pouring me some milk. "All it means is light hasn't responded to the dark just yet."

We returned to Aunt Katherine's church for a meal, and the tables shared memories about Grandma Paris, including the time she convinced Dad she had invented french toast and could have retired with all the money she made when she returned stateside with the recipe.

Some of my cousins had aged since I last saw them, like my classmates. Some of the boys had facial hair as thin as windowsill dust. Some of them had grown taller, some wider, some muscular. Some of us girls had changed. This time we didn't run around in the church's basement like during holiday get-togethers when we laughed and played billiards, table tennis, or hide-and-seek. A few times storms forced us down there for shelter with everyone else. An old organ sat in the corner. We all took turns playing it and singing. None of us were any good. Grandma Paris could play and often did with us kids down there. She would start with gospels, wanting us to get that Old Time Feeling, but after a

OCTOBER

few religious songs, she worked her way into jazz pieces, including the one Grandpa Ho kissed her to while dancing. We liked those movements a little more. She winked she did too.

"Is the organ still down there?"

"Take your cousins, if you go," Mom answered me.

I opened the basement door and flicked on the stairwell light, which broke up some but not all the dark angles and shadows always shaking me on my way down. The tables behind me laughed about another story. My cousins rushed the dessert trays while their parents grabbed fresh coffee pots. I didn't ask them to come with me. As I descended, all those sounds dwindled like cotton over a watch.

I shivered in the damp. Moths popped against the lamps, and I sidestepped puddles and cobwebs. And in a corner behind the pool and ping-pong tables glowed the organ's wood—as gold as a bird perched on a wire. I pulled the seat out, and the feet scraping echoed so much I waited for someone to come for me, but I settled by myself and cracked my fingers like Grandma Paris warmed up with scales. When we were all down here, we'd see how many could fit on the bench. The velvet was so slick it slid us off, and we made a game of who could sit the longest while the others muscled us off, which ended up in some hurt feelings and bruises but mostly laughter and ornery grit before we dug out hymnals and sing-alongs. I pushed back the cover. My hands hovered over the keys. I flipped through pages marked by

Grandma Paris, but not one spoke to me. Chairs and tables scooted upstairs and rattled the basement ceiling as folks sat closer to each other. Laughter and louder voices moved over me —between where I sat in silence and what she left behind.

When I reappeared, I walked back to my parents who smiled at me before I sat down and returned to stories. I had been in the cold, dark basement under the church for long enough, but the organ wasn't the only thing worth answering.

* * *

After Ray died, I didn't believe I could go on. Something else had to come for me and move me. The moment of his death changed me into someone else. My life lost intimate, important, and physical and emotional parts. Faith asked me for more, but I couldn't give anything else and certainly not myself. So many things other than faith helped me survive the months following his death. I clung to my senses the same way Ray clung to his beliefs. My faith had broken like a dirt road.

I wanted him back without his illness, but then I wanted him back with his illness just to have him back in my life. His death saddened me, but it did not terrify me. His body decayed. He wanted to hold on, but he also wanted to let go and follow letting go. Where it eventually led him, I used to know. My own death? For someone who prided herself on not being fearful, it did not terrify me until recently.

OCTOBER

That I have made it this far—outlasted so much, in a sense—that time is different, having passed by me, and yet early October grounds me and speaks more to me than my wrinkles, gray hair, extra weight, and bad joints. The leaves turn more color. Temperatures drop. Days shorten. A truck with a sign wired to its gate drove through our neighborhood. FIREWOOD 4 SALE. The church I walked into promoted, on bright neon-colored papers, Trunk or Treat, where Higher Grounds congregation will hand out candy from their cars. A sermon tying this tradition to Biblical teachings will be held beforehand. Games, activities, food, fun, and live music will follow. The dead never leave us, and we invite them into our lives.

After all these years of living here in Cole, I had not thought about any of this until Saul sent me the photo and the photo sent me to stand in a church advertised a few blocks from where I live.

As a young woman, I believed my prayers went unanswered, but I now believe they were answered but weren't made visible at the moment they were asked for but later when they could be understood. My place in the church was always small because a church and all it embodies is so very large. But I cannot escape faith and its motion of returning me to where I was and, at the same time, showing me where I could be. I had assumed faith was strength in accepting the visible while never letting go of the invisible, but it's an act of measuring the distance between bodies that different people and places told me about. It took me all these years to listen and to find out it never disappeared, only hibernated inside me, even in my moments of doubt when I was full of hope but not full of faith.

Not everyone knows how to live. But does everyone know how to die? These people and places blur as they move and are here in front of me—and have been the whole time. I am not scared. All these memories are because of everyone and everything I love. I welcome them all in. Whatever me drove me here to this church near where I live wanted me to step at least one foot inside, and I did, before stepping a little closer. And then I stopped. I know some of the reasons why I went in. The rest of them may not become clearer until further down the road. Where I am is enough.

5

Sherry Lynn's voice cracks on the phone as cars honk in the background. "Patty, I need help with the building out in Baxter. They didn't like who's been doing it. It should take a few hours. Three stories. We can divide and conquer. It could be long-term."

"How long?"

"Until we screw up like the people before us. I think we're looking at three months and then, if all goes well, a year."

"When do we start?"

"The fifteenth."

The calendar on my desk has so few hours for the library marked in red.

"OK. I'm in."

"Great. Thank you. Meet me at my place at seven that night, and we'll go from there. See you then."

Maybe it's the moonlight coming through the windows, but after hanging up the phone, the inside of my apartment grows. I move Ray's cane to open the curtains behind the computer. No clouds cover the sky. Neighborhood shadows are small. Davis and Karen scrabble around. It's a Tuesday, so they're probably watching something on PBS. Night silhouettes the headstones, witches, and spiders in our yard and Stubbs lounging on the front porch. The silence strengthens more. I mark SHERRY LYNN in the calendar's box. The middle of October will be here before I know it.

For her odd jobs, Sherry Lynn has hired folks other than me, but they left for other jobs, some of which were in Taylor. The younger adults she hired didn't mind the night schedules as long as they didn't interfere with social life, but eventually they would complain, want a break, or start asking about a pay raise or benefits. "I was like that once," she chuckled. She is about twenty years younger than me, and she is hipper to styles and trends than when I was her age, but she is not someone who spends a lot of money on those styles and trends. She puts her money where it needs to go.

Sherry Lynn owns A1 Cleaners, which services residents and businesses in the Tri-Valley, after discovering the franchise in an advertisement. She borrowed money from her family, the bank, and her ex. As a military vet, Gabe was able to secure more loans. They have a better-than-expected relationship after they divorced. He wants the best for the kids and her, which means not being together anymore. She said being close friends and business partners has been healthier for her than when they were a couple. They had their problems partly because they had married right out of high school when both families wanted them to be

OCTOBER

together for the birth of Ana Michelle—and for no reason other than that.

Before A1, Sherry Lynn was a beautician after she moved from Masons Corner, where she grew up, to Bon Air and then to Tubersville. She started SL Salon in their garage. She bought a mirror with drawers and a desk for her gear from a garage sale and had enough room for one chair she bought used. Gabe bolted it to the concrete floor, and he cracked most of the concrete. The bolts looked like shovels broken off and stuck in the ground. The chair swiveled in place, but he had installed it too far from the sink, which threw off their kitchen and washer waterlines. Sherry Lynn's clients stretched their heads for the basin, and the chair creaked every time. She was so worried her clients would fall over she propped the chair and their bodies on her legs while she shampooed and conditioned. "Bruises so big, black, and blue," she said, patting her big thighs.

I had my hair done by her as many times I could, putting a lot of miles on my car. She and I agreed to build up my brush of curls like a tower with every can of hairspray she had. We choked on the fumes trapped in the garage, calling them "beauty smoke," and joked they were like the dry ice in old black-and-white movies whenever a beautiful actress sashayed on screen for a scene everyone remembered. She added more clients and, at first, told Gabe to park his truck and their car in the driveway but then had him park in the street in order for her clients to have easy access to the garage because most of them were elderly or on disability, barely making ends meet, or they were folks who wanted to look like celebrities in magazines but who would never be asked to be in that magazine. But the truth, it seems, is only interesting to outsiders when it happens to someone who has to prove who they are and where they are even though they've been who they are and where they are when no one ever paid any attention before.

 Like all of her business ventures, Sherry Lynn contributes sweat equity, passion, and determination to A1. I've taken most of her jobs, not all, and the ones I took have padded me during the lean times after Ray. "I'm so sorry, Patty," she said. "But I'm also not doing this out of pity. I could use your help, and you could make some money." She called me her "workhorse," which is a nice compliment, given my old joints show their rust.

 We've cleaned modest houses, estates in the county, local offices, and historic buildings. We were the sole pick-up crew for the Sky Top Beer and Music Festival near Little Brother Mountain. We saw how folks take over an area they say is important to them as a place of nature and communion but never act that way. Glasses, cans, and trash lay all over. We were there long enough to hear the final few bands. Singing on the job got us through it all. Before we started cleaning up, Sherry Lynn and I took a few shots of whiskey provided by Battlefield Distillery. She swapped cleaning the factory for bottles of the

OCTOBER

special reserve released at Christmas—Mrs. Claus's Midnight Special. When the owner started out, he said, sipping with us, he relied on word of mouth, family and friends, his wife and children, hard work, and few dollars sitting in a business account. Sherry Lynn seemed to take that to heart.

We've prepped the rows of hotels and motels along the highway filling up before the Taylor Fair opens at the start of October. I've tried not looking at what guests leave behind, but clues and secrets always scatter about like puzzle pieces. One room had a stack of LPs in a plastic crate stuffed in the corner between the bed and the wall. Sherry Lynn and I thumbed through them. They were in fair condition. She was about to call the front desk and have the manager come for them when a young man, not more than eighteen, knocked on the door.

"Those are mine," he stuttered.

He was rail-thin, his face peppered with acne, and hadn't bathed in a while, his arms and clothes so dirty.

"Prove it," she said.

He rambled off the titles and described some of the covers. She slid the crate his way.

He snatched it and started for the door, but before he passed through, he turned around with tears in his eyes. "They're my mom and dad's. I wanted to teach them a lesson. They don't pay no attention to us." He hustled down the stairs and jumped in a car idling in the parking lot.

After Early Bird closed its doors, Gloria asked me to put in a good word with Sherry Lynn, but she got on the line at Downy & Sons Manufacturing in Reins. She lost a finger in a pressing machine. She said she missed the burns she got from the hot-grease splashes and the skillets Jimmy tossed around in order to get the food done real quick.

"Now when I flip somebody off because they irked me, it doesn't quite look the same," she said. "It's not even a half-flip!"

"What about your other hand?"

"That's not my power hand." She laughed before sniffling. "I miss him and you and all that."

"He was a good egg."

"R.I.P., Jimmy Wasson," we said.

As much as I've never wanted to be under the spell of money, the extra income from Sherry Lynn's latest offer will help. Temporary jobs paying hourly and never having insurance, benefits, or perks are like kudzu—taking over the places no one visits anymore. Growing up, we weren't poor like Ray's and Saul's families, but we weren't wealthy. When my girl cousins and I pierced our ears, we used safety pins to keep the holes open because we could not afford the jewelry the rich ladies wore. I laugh at the number of side gigs I've had because the permanent jobs that pay well—with the city, county, or state or as one of those traditional white-collar jobs—are very hard to come by.

"Try again in a few months," they always say. Months pass, but

OCTOBER

nothing opens up. Some of the places need extra help for the holiday rushes, but for the most part, jobs have been scarce and hard-earned for me, and they are scarcer and harder to get hold of now that I'm older.

    I walk from my apartment down to the end of the road where Ashbery Street runs into Cornell Lane. No cars are out, and it is so quiet I can hear my heart beat and my ears ring. The same doctor who told me to change my diet believed my hearing, in my old age, had deteriorated so much my brain created sounds my ears could no longer hear but, according to my brain, had to have in order to keep doing their job—listening for every high and low pitch and every vibration in the air, even if the pitch and the vibration were private, and because they were private, they created sounds for to you hear wherever you stood. Sounds so we don't have to be alone, I said to myself.

    I avoid tripping on the inflatable pumpkin, and following the strings of purple and orange lights, return through our yard of the dead, say goodnight to Stubbs, and although they can't see me, wave to Davis and Karen. I scoop my coffee for the morning. I fix my usual Sunday dinner of popcorn with a mix of salt and sugar sprinkled on top and an apple with peanut butter. I pour myself a tall glass of ginger ale on ice and flop onto the couch. *Been Down There Before*, my favorite radio program, plays old blues, country, and Americana on WCOL. I clean my dishes, brush my teeth, pull back my bedcover and sheets. I glance at calendar with its new red mark on the fifteenth and then at the computer. Sherry Lynn's message was my only one.

. . .

We load brooms, gloves, mops, buckets, and cleaning chemicals into Sherry Lynn's van. By the time we finish and plop ourselves in the seats, the time is almost eight. The sun set hours ago. The A1 Cleaners franchise gave Sherry Lynn additional decals for just about everywhere a space stuck out like blank paper. CONTACT US TODAY FOR A1 CLEANING! is the call to action. On the bottom left rear bumper, her faded franchise operating number is barely visible under grime and dents.

"Only one time has someone gotten my number and called headquarters about something I did they didn't like." She puts the van in drive. "This dude said I cut him off in traffic heading back from Suffolk Springs, but I was headed east that morning. It wasn't me. But that family up on Addison in that Twin Oaks neighborhood treated me like I was some kind of Cinderella help."

"The new-money part of town," I say, tightening my seatbelt when she turns the wheel hard right. "Big, new houses."

"They wanted me to clean up after their dogs had been in the yard. I said, 'That's not in the agreement you signed for. I would do it, but you didn't request that kind of service.' Not that I wanted to, but if it's requested and in writing, then sure, I would.

OCTOBER

I kindly reminded them they only wanted me to give the kitchen a good, solid once-over. Grease, food, whatever. They thought I was violating the contract. The wife refused to pay. She and I got into it. I said, 'Ma'am, I'd be happy to do what you want if we can sign another agreement. Won't take long.' She wanted none of that. Rich white women, I tell you what. She let go of that leash she had on her little husband who chewed me out."

"Lots of bees in their special bonnets."

"Tell me about it."

"Did you get in trouble?"

"Darren laughed it off and said I needed to keep my cool next time. I make them too much money for them to reprimand me too much." At a stoplight, she rests her elbow on the rolled-down window. "It's this thing I love and just how it is. I can sink myself, or I keep myself swimming. But the weight's all on me."

"That is so you."

"There's no other way."

As soon as the van's tires leave the county roads and hit the highway, she accelerates, which squashes me into my seat. We cruise past clusters of houses and the many farms out this way—mainly pecan farms but also alfalfa, corn, soybeans, hogs, cows, horses, emus, and Randolph's Sod Farm where legions of high-school boys from the Tri-Valley work during the summers and, after they graduate, sometimes stay on as full-time employees. The families of immigrants who moved into this area work there and at the other farms. The Randolph workers hunch over like roly-polys in these fields of greens—emerald, dark, or lime, depending on the season and age and blend of the grass—and they load giant tubes of grass, dirt-side facing out, onto pallets hoisted by a forklift that sets them onto a truck bed where another group of workers fastens them for delivery. All day they do this, dividing their time between the quadrants of dry, ready-to-go sod and the quadrants of sod soaked by sprinklers so large and long they look like metal aliens from a science-fiction movie. Davis worked there for a while, years ago, but the heat and the constant movement was too much for his back and allergies, although he never confessed to that. Karen told me many of the managers yelled at him. He covered his ears when he heard her say this to me. But he will remind Karen and me, "Once a Randy Boy, always a Randy Boy" and, with an animal smirk on his face, flex his biceps. He'll see former coworkers around town, and they'll hug and greet each other like brothers. Randolph's has been in business for seventy years, and with all the growth of houses and neighborhoods happening out here, they are poised for more. But for the rest of the farms and farmers on the outskirts of Cole, most aren't independent anymore—the ones that have survived this far. Big agricultural companies have subsidized and automated most of them.

 The night is so clear that when we reach the large hill near the exit for Baxter, the edges of Taylor's eastern suburbs twinkle in

OCTOBER

the distance. Further west of here, the land blurs and blends. Cole and Taylor thrive as though neither city boundaries nor county lines exist—and will continue to blur until, one day in the future, these two places once praised for being different no longer are and are instead held together by jobs and money more than by the people who live there.

    City Manager Michael J. Ferguson III has been saying the top priority has moved from sewage to jobs, which brought on expected puns—"What Stinks in Cole City Council?" "City Council Can Handle Number One but They Can't Handle Number Two"—after a *Cole Daily News* reporter discovered the city owes the state fines, which rack up per month, with enough numbers in them looking like professional athletes' salaries. Trey, as Ferguson III is professionally known—Trey Bomb as he is privately and, in some circles, publicly known because of his quarterback arm that sent the Cole Spartans to the state playoffs thirty years ago—says the city has a ten-year jobs-investment program. "Let the good citizens of Cole decide what is best for them," he's said again and again. He knows Cole so well, which is part of the tragedy waiting to unfurl, and when it does, we'll have these heart-to-heart conversations on the streets, at city council meetings, and in the media about what went wrong and how we can grow from our mistakes, which will last until the next unfurling. How did we not see this coming? we'll ask ourselves. And the answer, as it always is, was in front of us the whole time.

WILLIAM AUTEN

    The van accelerates, but everything surrounding us slows until the land stands still as sharp as a black-and-white photo. So many SOLDs in big bold letters cover many FOR SALEs—acres, offices, or houses like a straight shot to a destination through patchworks of fields, trees, and roads splitting off the main highway. Out there, animals move around, sleep, eat, drink, watch us fly by. Their eyes glow in the light—large and small animals children would want to see or touch, to carry these animals back to their homes and into their beds where they would no longer need to dream of those animals greeting them during sleep. Before disappearing underneath stars and the night sky, other signs glow in the van's headlights: TAYLOR FAIR and MISS LEDBETTER'S HAUNTED HAYRIDE AND PUMPKIN PATCH MAZE.

    Another land appears alongside the land outside the van and cruising under our feet. With the window cracked, it seeps into me—the land that lies in Saul's photo. Somewhere in its exact location the photo's land is as tangible as the land Sherry Lynn and I pass through, yet it captures not one single moment but a universal and unavoidable moment filled with history and people, all of which and all of whom are frozen in a time and a place but yet move across years and across borders, holding neither a message nor a sign but one mortal detail as bright as a lantern shining on its findings. That land in the photo comes to me, but I cannot enter this land or find Saul in it.

OCTOBER

Like the land the van passes through, the land in Saul's photo has a horizon and rolls and dips in the distance, giving contour to the land. The photo extends into the landscape, and the landscape extends into the photo—one landscape seen and felt by our senses, and the other, in Saul's photo, a place to rest finally, a still shot of life coming and going. One land is *into and present*. The other land will remain *out of and soon*. If I could hold each land side by side, I would see two landscapes coming in and then going out, but I cannot separate the lands because they are inside and outside of me—they are mine—two distinct lands overlapping as I cross through them. One passes in front of me and on my way to work, while the other landscape waits for me where I live.

Turning at the Baxter exit, we hit the long stretch of woods and then the road taking us to our destination. The building is up ahead, the van keeps moving, but memory becomes the greater engine. To love and to be loved is to continue life. But outliving someone you love and moving on is also survival. These landscapes hold the remains of my life and share the same space. If only the land could untangle me from the thickets of other times and other places. I am between a start and a finish, the limits of what I knew and the edges of what I could know, as though moving in between would erase where I am and where I've been, until I stood in the middle of that unfolding sequence. As though the landscape needed me to be here, shuffling around until I found something waiting for me to find it—and I would have to remain here until I did.

・・・

From the horizon, the building rises. Lights shimmer on the fat, square building, as though invisible hands shaped its metal skeleton and fleshed its surface with thousands of panes of glass like mirrors. In the darkness out here, it is a source of light, a block of washed-out brightness sitting in a woodsy area carved out by concrete, electricity, and plumbing and surrounded by trees with changed leaves. The road we took to reach here disappears. A few barns and farmhouses spread around the building but are nearly unseen because of the forests. Rumor has it Cole and the county will partially fund a bus stop out here, after Taylor's GoGreen initiative. But the sky still dominates and is so clear the stars can be counted. And there are many to move under.

The building houses a tech company creating jobs, stability, and local taxes and revenue after the economic crisis of several years ago, but it has taken as long to reach this point. The empty shell sat after the recession forced out the first occupant—a northeast company planned on moving its customer-service center here—and it fell into the hands of Anthony Eubanks, a multi-millionaire whose family once had connections to the area. Tony, he insisted on being called, was nostalgic for a place he had

OCTOBER

been told about but had never been to—having lived, been educated, and worked states away where their accent is as plain to us as ours jars them—and wanted to transform the building into a modern-day spa and retreat. "Lots of potential and bringing unlimited imagination to the depths of the soul," he always said in interviews. Cole city council weighed their options, and although a few council members and several citizens voiced their concerns against such a maneuver, they gave him the green light. But the economic downturn hit a new low and forced Tony to abandon his project. All this frenzy kept *Cole Daily News* reporters and editors busy, and it kept the local shops and restaurants abuzz. Everyone talked about it, had an opinion, and swore they had seen this disaster coming, and if only the city had listened to them, more economical storms would not have gathered.

"That's what they get for following their wallets."

"Money is root of all evil."

"Greed and pride gets you every time."

"Community before egos."

Tony eventually sold the building to the current resident. ARK is headquartered in California, which is so far away from here it remains to some folks the myth of the Golden West, wondrous in diverse landscapes, and beautiful people, but to other folks, it's a shoulder shrug of Who Cares Where It Is—I'm Here With Everything And Everyone I Know And Don't Need To Be Anywhere Else.

"Back there," Sherry Lynn says, throwing her chin toward the short side of the building when our van rolls into the parking lot.

Reaching the service-entry doors, she swipes her card. The green light flashes. We gather our gear and stand near an elevator. Sherry Lynn fumbles through her keys and finds the one that stalls it open while we lug our things inside, which takes us longer than we thought. Hauling the heavier equipment demands both of us. Pains needle my elbows, knees, and back. I drink some water. A long night is ahead.

Once we're stuffed in the elevator, Sherry Lynn twists her key again. Before the doors close, the parking lot's brightness highlights three cars sprinkled here and there—people working late or who, for whatever reason, left their cars.

On the third floor, the elevator doors ping open, and the stars are the first things I see, not the executive suites filled with leather furniture and big desks or, at the end of the hall, a conference room with a large television screen and mounds of phones. Most of the third floor is blacked out—no overhead lights and no office lights on. Nothing but stars twinkling outside the windows and over fields, tips of trees, and concrete.

We float in that world separating where we stood on the ground and the panes of glass placed between us and the smudges of light and dark. Astronauts rocketed into space cannot touch the stars, but they are closer than when they stood on Earth. Far away, the stars hold all the wishes cast there, long after

OCTOBER

the wisher has vanished. We turn on the lights, and we are left with our tasks and solitary reflections as the stars blink away from the glass like a stage trick.

Sherry Lynn unpacks some of the gear. My joints are better but not by much. She is a strong gal and thick in her carriage. She lifts bulky things from the ground like they are filled with air. Her mom had her when she was sixteen and barely graduated high school while working for the armory out in the county. Her dad was a mechanic and a big teddy bear, but as Gabe told her when they were dating, he let Gabe know where Gabe stood especially if he did anything dishonorable to Sherry Lynn or her family name. "Well, then don't do anything dishonorable," she said.

After we organize ourselves and start at the far end of the office suites, Sherry Lynn asks, "So how you been?"

"Can't complain too much." I open a package of heavy-duty gloves. Once on, they are so heavy on my hands, which have more pronounced blue veins and thinner skin under the artificial office lights.

"I've been thinking about you. Sorry I haven't checked in until I had this job."

"Don't worry about it. We pick up like riding bikes. Besides everyone has their life to live."

"How're your neighbors?" She piles her hair under a red bandana and ties it off at the base of her neck where her tattoo jumps out—a cross and the names of her kids.

"We spent last weekend setting up our Halloween decorations."

"Y'all go to town on those."

"We're slowing down." I double-check my gloves. "I'm slowing down. But it's fun and one of the things we love to do with each other."

"My kids were ready back in September. Ana Michelle is ready to leave everything about Cole. And the more she complains, bless her heart, everyone else is ready to help her pack." The broom handle slumps in her hands. She slides on her mask. "Taylor, she reminds all of us, is the place to be if you're cool and hip and 'want a real life.'" Sherry Lynn throws up air quotes. "Not like Cole. She said the lunches at school look better than her future in Cole."

"Just you wait. Someday Cole will be the place to be. Everyone will want to leave but only because people will be moving here. No one will ever complain about being stuck here."

"I would kill to see that day. I hope to see it," she says, laughing. "And I'll be honest with you, when it happens, I'll probably be a grumpy old woman who will complain about all those strangers moving in here and ruining a good place with charm and character with their fancy, hifalutin ways. But I won't be moving. My butt's going nowhere."

"Taylor's already doing that."

OCTOBER

"They are, those sons a guns!" She grabs a roll of trash bags and empties the wastebaskets near us. "How's your friend? Made plans to see each other yet? Maybe a date, some good Italian food and wine somewhere nice?"

"As far as I know, he's fine."

Sherry Lynn gives me a look while I keep dusting.

"If I had a dollar for every time I asked that myself, I wouldn't be here. I'd retire and cut you in on it."

We laugh.

"He sent a photo and has promised to send a translation about it, but that's been it. That was September."

"I thought you two were tight."

"I guess something came up."

"Something or *someone*?" Her eyes sparkle with the look she throws my way.

"His own life took him different places."

Sherry Lynn scoots back a nice chair with multiple levers on it for adjusting nearly every part of the lower body and then pushes her broom under it. "Maybe Ray stopped it from happening. He's watching out. His ghost's watching you."

"That's sounds like him. Jealous in a good way."

For a second, she stops sweeping. "I'm sorry. I know you liked spending time with your friend. He seemed to come into your life when you needed someone like that. Saul, right?"

I nod yes.

"What was the photo he sent?" She dangles her forefinger before slowly stiffening it.

"No," I chuckle back, blushing.

"Did you send him one? You have nice big boobs."

"It's of a place he said he had been to and it struck him so much he had to pass it on to me. He said I would understand it like he did. And then silence." I load a bucket with cleaning solution and lower my face mask. "He later said the main grave marker in the photo has an inscription he'll send the translation for. The inscription means more than the photo." I stir the mop inside the bucket. The fumes creep up and irritate me a bit. It's been a while since I last did this. "But he also said the words can't be the same without the place."

"What'd you say?" Sherry Lynn yells, having had slid down to another part of the hall.

"The words on the stone!"

"Rome?"

"Close. Funny you should say that. The photo is in Europe."

"Show it to me when we're at your place. I'd like to see it. And then I'll send him an email telling him to get his act together and start treating you better. I'll tell him where all the good Italian restaurants are in Taylor. I'll do some of the work for him because God forbid he has to. Or else, I'll sic my dad on him."

OCTOBER

I laugh and smile more to myself than to her, but she nods, and then in silence, we move our separate ways, turn everything spotless, and put everything back in order for the next day.

After an hour passes, Sherry Lynn says, "Do you want to head on down to the second floor and start there? I can finish up here, and then we'll meet on the first floor and knock it out. And then we're done." She looks at her watch. "Not too bad. I'm guessing twelve thirty. Maybe one at the latest. We could still make it in time for a late-night drink before O'Malley's closes."

"I need my beauty rest." I jiggle my short white curls in the air. "Divide and conquer."

"Yes, ma'am. Chippin' away like the ol' gals we are." She picks up a long-handled duster. "Thank you, Patty."

I make my way past the far-end blocks of executive suites, turn for the elevator, and with my share of the cleaning supplies on a rolling cart, head down to the second floor. Leaning against the inside of the elevator, I rest my hip. I want to massage my hands, but I don't want to take off the gloves. The chemicals cling to me like a wet mane.

On the second floor, the offices multiply and twist on each other. The walls of the open-air cubicles look like steeplechases tucked so tightly with sharp corners and very little space to start or finish they blur together as though any employee on a whim can slide between any of the stations and fuss and fidget, stick their noses where they may not need to belong. Computers of all shapes and sizes crowd every desk—some with two or three monitors. Everyone can watch you working or not working. Everything you have in this space belongs to your colleagues.

Near a break room with vending machines and a small dark space at the back, as deep as a closet, a sign says

THE QUIET ROOM CAN BE USED FOR MEDITATION, CALM PRACTICES, STRESS-RELIEF, SELF-CARE, AND NAPS FOR NO MORE THAN 15 MINUTES. PLEASE PUT PILLOWS AND BLANKETS BACK WHERE YOU FOUND THEM AND LEAVE THE ROOM IN A CLEAN, PEACEFUL, TIDY WAY FOR THE NEXT HUMAN. THANK YOU! IF YOU HAVE ANY QUESTIONS, EMAIL OR SET UP A QUICK IM CHAT WITH GWEN OR ONE OF OUR INTERNS.

I take a peek. The room is so bare cleaning it is pointless. I leave it alone as well as the room next to it where three of its four walls are dedicated to giant racks stuffed with blinking lights and buzzing with electricity. I do not want to mistakenly turn off or on something. A light is on in the office at the far end of the right-side of the floor. No other offices are lit.

A man in that office stops vigorously typing on his keyboard. He snaps his head at me. The skin underneath his bloodshot eyes are damp and puffy. "Hello," his voice scratches out.

"I am so sorry. I didn't mean to disturb you. We're the cleaning crew."

OCTOBER

Sniffling and clearing his throat, he says, "Not a problem. You didn't bother me." He wipes his face. "Come in if you need to. Let me get out of your way." He stands up, smooths his tie, and props against the doorframe of the adjacent office. Legs crossed at his ankles, arms tight against his chest, he stares at the tile floor.

"Thank you." With my broom and duster in hand, I head in.

"How long have you been doing this?"

"We got here close to nine. It's been…" My blurry eyes look around for the time.

"No, this." He points to the rolling cart of supplies between us.

"My friend hires me whenever she needs help. She's upstairs. But she may be on the first floor now."

"You were up in the executive area?"

"We were."

He sighs heavily, glances at me and then at the floor, and juts out his jaw far enough to expose his teeth and swollen red gums. The rest of his body tightens like a rope. Slightly above-average height and dark-haired with gray at his temples and on the jawline of his unshaven beard, he could be a runner or a cyclist because of his slim frame. His face is gaunt and smaller in comparison to his long limbs. His cheeks are flush with the triangular downslope of his chin. He wears a plain white dress shirt, a blue-and-black-striped tie, and a pair of loafers the color of wood coated in dark amber shellac. His small square eyes, combined with the softness of his face, hold me and grow because of something or several things he wants to say but can't or won't. He smiles slightly and stares at the space above the floor.

"All finished," I say, walking back to my cart.

"Thank you." He uncrosses his arms and ankles, raises his head, and walks toward his office. He pivots his chair at the computer and makes the sound he made earlier—a sound like he was going to speak but another breath lifted him from the depth he was headed into. His fingers hover over the keyboard, but he does not type, and for an instant, alongside this anonymous man, Dad tinkers at his workbench, Ray sings a song at the cabin, and Saul clicks send.

The chair swivels, and the man looks at me like someone who wants to leave but cannot. "It's a good way to end it." He nods and sniffles again. "It's my last night here."

"Well, I hope it's a fresh start."

"They laid me off."

"I'm so sorry to hear that."

"I have two girls at home. One's a senior in high school. The other's in eighth grade. The senior has plans for college, but now I don't know. And the eighth-grader, well, she likes clothes, books, music, but her allowance might be coming to an end."

OCTOBER

"I had an allowance once. I was supposed to do this and that...the garbage, help my mom in the garden, take care of Beeker."

The man smiles.

"We weren't sure what Beeker was. Part-spaniel, maybe, part-lab, probably. He had this for a head, that for a body, and something else for his tail and feet. He was cuddly and chubby, not much of a hunting dog for my dad or uncles, but we all loved him. I got a few dollars for all that. I mostly spent it on the same things your youngest does."

"I never had an allowance. I had jobs. Mowed lawns, roofed houses. I fixed computers in college. I had to get paychecks, not an allowance."

"Those are good skills."

Looking down and then up at me, he says, "I was going to run away tonight. I was the last one here. No one else knows I've been laid off. The execs know." He throws his eyes up to the third floor. His jaw juts again, but his lips do not reveal as much of his canines or red gums as earlier. "But no one else knows."

"Why would you run away?"

He swallows hard. "I have bills and mortgages. My wife can't work. She's on disability. Horrible migraines. My family means the world to me."

"Listen, it's a set-back. You'll find something. Or something will find you. It's there. You just can't see it yet."

He clicks his keyboard a few times. A photo of his family stands near the corner of his desk under which lies a box he started putting some of his things into. In the photo, he and his family huddle together on the edge of a boat. The mast sticks up behind them, and the deck rail wraps around them. It's hard to tell if he is younger, but his hair is a little longer and flops over his ears and face while the ocean air twists up the back. His arms reach around his wife and daughters. Leaning in, his wife wears large dark sunglasses with lenses the size of small plates. Her hair corkscrew down to her chin. She is dressed in long sleeves and pants, the flowing black fabric protecting her from sunlight. Her head rests on his shoulder, and bliss fills her smile. His oldest girl has a mouthful of braces, hair down to her waist, straight and thin and billowing in the wind, and acne reddens her cheeks and forehead and pulls her face from the camera until it captures her wanting to be seen but not looked at. And wearing a hodgepodge of colors and designs for a shirt and shorts, like an old country quilt stitched with whatever patterns were at hand, his youngest daughter stretches her arms in front of them, her legs doing the splits, and she scrunches her face like a cartoon.

"I think I've seen you around town. The library?"

I smile and nod. "Yes, I work there too."

"It's a good library. My daughters love it. We go there almost every Sunday afternoon."

OCTOBER

"I haven't been working there on Sundays in a while. I used to quite a bit."

"What are you doing here?"

"Income."

"Are you hiring?"

"She has been getting busier. I can say something to her."

"No, it's OK." His hands brush me away as he blushes and lowers his head.

"What did you do here?"

"I managed projects, which is a big way of saying I sat in this chair at this desk in this office for more than ninety hours a week, a lot on weekends, got paid fairly handsomely, but was mostly told by my bosses I should put in more effort. 'Can you try harder for us in this quarter?' was their favorite phrase."

"I've never worked for a big company like this. There aren't many here in Cole. This is one of a few, but they're growing."

"It'll all be different before you know it."

"It seems as though so much has already changed."

"And yet so much stays the same." He finds the cover for the box.

"It would be nice to have more than a job for knowing who we are."

"Sounds good on paper, but in practice, I don't think this world is set up for that, if it ever was." After breathing deeply, he says, "I should let you get back to work. I'm sorry for keeping you."

"No, it's fine. I'm glad we had a chance to talk." I push my cart a little further down and start cleaning again. I wipe my eyes with my wrist where the glove does not cover it. I head back to his office. "Listen, I know we don't know each other, but I just want to say to you that things will turn around. They do, especially when you don't see it right away. All of it. Not tonight and not tomorrow but someday soon. And you should be there to see it when it happens."

He smiles, nods, and loads a few more things into the box under his desk.

I look behind me at the single light of his office glowing in the hall before returning to the rest of my work and then back down to the first floor. Sherry Lynn and I smile at each other while I dodge some of the spots on the tile she mopped. I roll my cart and supplies to one part of the lobby, which a tall wraparound glass shapes in a half-circle. Beyond that glass, the van and the three cars sit in the parking lot and also beyond the glass sits the stretch of fields, dark sky, and thick bed of stars.

• • •

Paintings and sculptures, computer screens, magazines on glass tables, and a coffee-and-juice bar and cafeteria at the end of one of the wings line the lobby. Waiting for whatever reason you

OCTOBER

were here—job interview, a proposal, or to meet someone who worked here—would not bore you. So many stimulations bounce and flash inside these glass walls, and if that doesn't occupy you, then, if it were daytime, an unobstructed view of the outside with birds, the sun, and flowers near the entrance opens to you. But the night and all its space spread in front of me.

ARK's giant name and boat logo on the wall behind the desk leaps out because their shiny letters change colors depending where I stand as I clean around the reception desk. Signs on the other walls say the building is environmentally friendly and was built with recycled materials, some of which are from the area. I squint, trying to find exactly what, and chuckle at rusted machinery and equipment, sap-ridden trees with cumbersome knots, and a battalion of mosquitoes and ticks stuffed somewhere in here. One plaque notes twenty skilled laborers contributed to the construction, and the words refer to the twenty folks in the area who were hired for this work as part of the deal to bring the company here but, once the job was done and the doors opened, were let go.

Important people walk into this lobby and, by extension, into Cole, which makes me snicker. Who would fly in a bone-rattling prop plane onto our one weed-infested runway at our dinky Tri-Valley Airport, with farm animals, a highway, and patchworks of fields as the sights along the way, after landing at Taylor International Airport, rent a car or have a car waiting for them, and end up here? Did they think this was some other place more recognized in some other part of the country?

Sherry Lynn and I finish up the main floor and lobby and exit the building. She double checks the service doors are closed and the light switches to red, but she runs back in and grabs a bottle she left on the reception desk.

Shaking her head, she says, "Strike one for us. The security cameras will have a heyday with me running back in there. I'll have to beg them for more business now."

It's a little after one in the morning. We load our gear back into the van, and while it idles, she checks her phone. Her mom left a message about Ana Michelle watching an R-rated movie with her friends and not studying for her biology test.

"I wonder which part she feels guilty about?" She asks me with a laugh. "She is just like me at that age." She stresses each of her words with big exhales. Her seatbelt clicks in place.

"Hold on." I get out of the van and walk toward a dark green, nearly black, area between the building and the parking lot. The stars are most prominent over here where the office and parking-lot lights do not reach. Nothing has been built yet, but a FOR SALE sign is nearby. I walk further into the space. The tall grass gives way to short sprigs and the smell of wild mint.

Four deer cross behind the trees in front of me. They leap and scamper deeper into the dark woods. I turn around. The building's second floor is all dark. The van and, now, two cars

OCTOBER

remain in the parking lot. The third one left at some point. I pinch myself to make sure none of my time with the man up there was a dream. If I could pocket all this twinkling light for him, I would because I have not wanted to be alone with the present. Where else am I to go? But what if I am right where I am supposed to be—and the constellations tell me this? What if the sky leads to a path worth taking and that path leads to exactly under my feet? What else—who else—am I to pass? What else—who else—is to pass me?

 Starting over is as common as the changing seasons, but the stars will not follow me as much as they will simply be wherever I end up, which could be here and now, standing in the middle with what the light shines upon, or somewhere else I have to reach. The stars are consistent, and they are wherever I go—be it for money, memory coming back or breaking down, or many loves strengthening life. The stars are present and follow me like words, even as they hide inside the blue sky of day. But they cannot take me back to the moments I had. They light what is in front of me so I can see straight ahead and let go of so much in order to get there.

 Everyone I've ever known has stopped to look at stars with me. <You'd be too much buried inside yourself to not see them.> Saul wrote. And on our hikes along the Chickataw, Ray and I found constellations telling us where we were—and when —like a string pulled tightly between hands on opposite sides of a gap. And when you stand under stars, the whole world opens up. Time doesn't stop or slow down, and you can neither leave your troubles nor can they leave you, but standing under starlight levels them until small shoots of joys rise like fires among the ashes. The stars for the man I met on the second floor of the building are the same stars in the sky over me, and they will clarify the distance he has to shorten while finding answers to his questions. They may be closer than he realizes.

6

BIG OAKS says the sign in the Chickataw River Preserve. It's my favorite trail. The sound of river increases as I leave the parking lot behind me and the woods grow in front of me. Plenty of those trees are the kings out there, but they aren't the only ones sticking out halfway through the month. Red maples and dogwoods, yellow cottonwoods, yellow hickories, orange sweetgums. A grove of pines near a bend signals I've left the entrance and, with the twisting of silence, water, and leaves, am farther from my start. Everything is ready to shed more of summer and move deeper into the late-afternoon light of fall.

Walking is my preferred exercise, and I prefer exercising in the morning, but working on the Baxter building with Sherry Lynn and setting up the decorations with Davis and Karen weeks ago did a number on my body, and every morning since has been like setting a snail in molasses and telling it to giddy up. My arthritis tightens every joint. The sun reaches noon faster than it takes for me to get loose, and when I finally do, like today, the day's nearly gone. I shuffle before walking—a few fat squirrels are more agile than me. But I need to move, be outside, and get my pulse up. Ray and I tried a personal trainer down at the Cole Rec

Center, but we didn't like that as much as walking. I've gotten use to walking alone, and once I get going, my pace breaks just enough I can cross this off my list for the day. As Mom said, "Women don't sweat. We glow."

<That is the same thing my momma and all my ex-wives and girlfriends said. Course, my momma is in my humble opinion ten times stronger than any woman after her because she never had the stuff we have nowadays. All these cushy caves we have like we never want to face any of the many many dragons out there in the world. But for exercise she was always out there with my dad working the land. Best way to exercise the heart and head as far as I'm concerned.>

<I agree. Do you like to exercise?>

<I did my middle age man thing where I lifted as much weight as I could because God forbid I was going to "do cardio" and got so bulky somebody should've held up a mirror to my thick face and told me to back off or else I'd end up onstage at the state fair. Which I then did. I started running. I did a 5k then a half marathon then a full. Pretty soon everyone started calling me Slim Saul.>

<Funny, but that's also great.>

<Thank you. But I got bored with that and went into cycling. But not for me. Although I found a group of old folks like me. We called ourselves the Grayhounds because it was a bunch of old guys and gals who chased everything running by them as

OCTOBER

though if it got away from us we'd never see it again. It was fun to do, and I got enough road out here for miles and miles, but I'd rather sit for hours and hours in a horse saddle or taking one of my cars out for long drive. Clop clop or vroom! That fiberglass seat underneath me on that bike did a number on my you know what. I got to keep my pipes in working order especially now I'm hitting the twilight years. But I tell you what I did so much hiking over there in Europe. It was perfect. We hiked at least ten miles a day, a lot along the Danube. And when we came across that spot in the photo I sent you…wow. It was a perfect day. Sunshine. Good temp. Spring. Just a few patches of snow. Not a soul in sight. So to speak. We had to climb some elevation to get there, and after we did, I had that high folks talk about when they're in nature and they've been running or hiking. That spot was there. That stone marker was there. Those words on it were there. That weather and the presence of something so larger than yourself. You can't miss something like that. When they come they come. And they always come when you weren't expecting it and when you needed it.>

    Late March through mid-September provide enough light in mornings and afternoons out here along the Chickataw. My walks could never end during those months. I don't have to set much aside before the rest of the day turns to night. October and these earlier sunsets, however, change the forest's light from bright to fuzzy yellow like a fire behind its smoke. Darkness comes on quickly, and walking alone and further into the woods can be frightening but not in the sense of being attacked or robbed. Crimes like that are rare in Cole, and the trail, winding and crumbling into the river, can be treacherous if you don't pay attention. Many years ago, some teenage lovers seriously injured themselves after falling from the cliffs overlooking the river, but they had been drinking and, once they recuperated, ended up more as the talk of parties and the halls of Cole High than as warnings. This unfortunate event happened on Valentine's Day—the nights still long, emotions like toys. Stumbling in the dark is easy, even with someone next to you and holding onto you, as though so much in a life is balanced because of someone else.

 Ray and I had a good hike when we had our get-away at the mountain cabin. For someone recovering from his first bout with cancer, he had so much energy, like a switch flicked on and charged every part of his body. When he relapsed, we walked along the Chickataw but could go only so far. Everything about his body hurt—lungs, hips, knees, muscles. His palms fell to his knees, his body stooped, his breathing calmed, and I waited for him to stand up until we walked again, both of us smiling as we held hands. Even his skin talked back to him. I often helped him back to the car. In his final days, I was his only means of standing up on this trail. Our turnaround point shrank week by week until we staggered from the parking lot to the start of the trail marked by the bench with the plaque on its back.

OCTOBER

GIFT OF MRS. HARTZLER'S SECOND GRADE CLASS – COLE ELEMENTARY – THANK YOU FOR TEACHING US – SEE YOU IN HEAVEN.

After Ray passed, I stopped walking but had to start again. I walked in the afternoons or whenever I needed—anything to get out of our old house or my apartment. My mileage doubled, tripled. I lost fifteen pounds. I was the leanest I had been in decades, but I wasn't healthy. Ray didn't care if I carried extra weight or weighed 100 pounds sopping wet with cinderblocks in my pockets. One night, standing in the bathroom mirror, my body was youthful, but my face continued sliding. But sliding toward what? My veins, skin, and muscles were disconnected from my heart, which, although was inside me, underneath bone and tissue and between my lungs, fed and connected everything else in my body. But exercise, the so-called Elixir of Life purported by a variety of folks, never hoisted back my body's sliding parts. Several of the library's patrons and ladies I work with and some of those magazines I organize in periodicals swear caffeine's natural benefits can reserve, or at least slow down, the signs of aging, but I do not know what or who to believe. Sometimes those studies are reversed quicker than a spooked horse. But if my cups of coffee provide nothing more than the happiness of a daily ritual, then that's all right with me. Not enough coffee or makeup in the world can change how I look and feel.

In all the years of walking here along the Chickataw, my path has not changed. I joke to myself the boot marks in the mud and dirt are mine, not another hiker's, even if the prints are larger or smaller than mine because I have not wavered from the beginning, middle, or end. My turnaround point is two miles in from the parking lot and where the trail goes over the hills to the left and under the first set of electrical towers the county built a few years ago for the new neighborhood abutting the preserve.

By Cole's standards, the houses are mansions or, with their modern colors, bright lights, and landscaped yards, residences that a magazine would promote. The neighborhood's land has private trails, and once outside the fence line, join public trails, they are so finely manicured they belong in a movie about flawless characters in a spick-and-span city.

The tops of chicken wires in the homeowners' neighborhood garden glisten in morning or afternoon light when I pass, and in spring, the flowers and vines spiral onto the trail until the landscaping crew cuts them back. The abundance of daisies and wildflowers smother the NO TRESPASSING and PRIVATE PROPERTY signs prompting the rest of us where to walk and remind us access to the garden is for members of Rivers Edge Estates, most of whom are white-collar professionals driving into and out of Taylor on workdays. On my morning walks, couples

OCTOBER

and families pile into the same car or into separate cars, like time-lapsed videos of fans filling seats at a football game. On my afternoon walks, their cars pull into the garages like airplanes arriving at gates—one by one as scheduled. The people who live in those houses live in my town, but were I to run into them on the streets of downtown Cole or at any of our community events, I would not know any of them, and they would not know me.

Little things during my walks out here have surprised me or caught my attention, but I don't carry a camera. As much I'd like something extraordinarily beautiful to startle me, I have to focus where I step. Tripping on divots or exposed roots, bruising myself, skinning my knees and hands—I have learned the hard way but keep coming back. My car trunk now carries a first-aid kit, but one day, it won't be enough. I'll be too old and brittle for wrapping a bandage and slathering on wound ointment, and folks who'll find me, or what's left of me, won't know I was out and about on the trail like an old gal with some legs left under her saddle, not some senile senior lost or kicked out by the sturdier citizens of Cole who couldn't put up with my gibbering and wandering, like those old villages purging anyone who can't keep up in mind, body, or soul. "Go on and take your looks! I was out here on purpose! I tied my own shoes, dressed myself, and put my wrinkled derrière out here because I wanted to!" I'd like to shout to them—now and, if I'm bones and worm and buzzard food, in the future. Besides, what's an old gal like me supposed to do? Sit at home in my recliner and cry? Pout because I can't go the number of steps I once did or would like to? Or worry about the number of steps I do add up but could lose a little more every time I come out here? What good does all that do when trails that took Ray and me around that bend of rocks and big trees up there, that curve down to the water, or that sycamore grove behind me where we saw an eagle and hummingbirds the summer before his first bout with cancer, have a beginning and an end but loop wider and wider when I'm on them?

And today, everything around me grabs my attention—the birds, evening coming on over the water and between the trees, the air cooling. The tumble of the Chickataw startles me when the trail hooks me closer to the water. In the distance, on the other side of the river, a figure moves in and out of the branches and crunches the ground. I have seen deer out here, but I have never seen one by itself. Pamphlets at the preserve's entrance talk about foxes, groundhogs, skunks, and other usual forest suspects. Tall enough to be a human, the shadow creeps close to the river's edge and waits for me to see it before disappearing.

· · ·

During my senior year in high school, a boy I loved tried to kill himself at one of the bridges crossing the Chickataw. We knew each other since first grade. Robbie's father was a railroad

OCTOBER

engineer, as had been his father's father, and the joke around town was Mr. Schmidt delivered more families and all of my classmates than Dr. Harrison, Cole's main pediatrician at the time. His mother's family had been in the area for generations, rumored to arrive because the patriarch was on the run from authorities after a botched bank robbery he claimed he was forced to be part of but decided otherwise because of his moral conscience rekindling at the last minute. Martha was a community staple, well known in social circles and for aiding historical preservations, but she was very shy and stayed out of the limelight—more so after the cops found Robbie on the ledge of Benson Bridge.

From his father, Robbie inherited raven-colored hair, a narrow face and chin, and eyes as big and amber as whiskey, and like Robert Sr., he looked younger than his age. He was slightly taller than average height and more broad shouldered than most of the boys at Cole High. He tried basketball, baseball, and wrestling. He was told he threw like a girl, his legs were scrawny, or he wasn't man enough to overthrow and pin another man to the wrestling mat. He loved science and reading, which he shared with his mother, and yet he was never recognized for his academics, unlike other students who left Cole with their ribbons, achievement awards, and scholarships at colleges and universities. Robbie made mostly Bs and Cs, and pursuing grades snuffed out his curiosity and froze him during tests. He was someone, once his demeanor pulled you in, you wanted to be around as much as possible because he scrapped together pursuing a life outside of the life he had been given.

Mom said Robbie had a demon, which all families have, not only Robbie's, and pass onto their children, which is never their fault but something they have to face at some point.

"What's ours?" I asked her.

"Bad case of the bottle on your daddy's side. Anxious thoughts stop you in your tracks on mine."

Robbie would shift from being the sweetest, most quiet, sensitive boy into being lost in a night without stars or exit roads. He tried controlling it, but he needed help moving from point to point. Because of his behavior, people assumed he was antisocial. When Robbie lost his temper, everything and everyone around him felt it. He sulked, and boys who sulk in high school halls spend so much of their adolescence defending themselves. He had good in him. But I could not stop any of this. My parents said we were responsible for asking God to show us how to care for and help people like him in need.

Contrary to what my classmates and their teasing suggested, I never dated Robbie. I did not love him romantically. I loved him as the Bible taught us to love one another—love is for everyone and everyone is worthy of love. But teenagers being teenagers, everyone I knew, like my cousins at Grandma Paris's funeral, changed when puberty hit—hierarchies were established. By the

OCTOBER

time you entered Cole High, you had to know your place, and if you didn't, you had to find one. Robbie was there for me when it became clear I was not at the top of the hierarchy, and I was there for him when it became clear high school would roughen him for four years. And to have a boy interested in me when I was not a cheerleader, popular, or rich made me slightly more visible, seen, and heard in school. Robbie told me I was his one true friend. I prayed every day he made it through school unscathed, and mostly he did until the last semester of our final year.

Every day between third and fourth periods, near the lockers, the circle of boys from the football team waited for him. He was an easy target, and my peers were cruel—the same peers who sat in church pews, sang hymns, and listened to sermons and whom I had known as long as I had known Robbie.

Robbie had to walk a path crossing Tommy Gorton, who was one of the less skilled and less decorated but more vocal football players who loomed over everyone. He said the usual things boys like that say to boys like Robbie. Tommy's folks were regulars at the grocery store where Dad worked, but after the incident with Robbie, they stopped coming in. They went to a butcher on the other side of town but returned to Dad's store and ordered if he wasn't working.

Robbie convinced himself he should not avoid the young men who picked on him. If he could show them he was not afraid, then they would change their ways. Joining the football team was his solution. He talked to Coach McGraw, who told him anyone who is willing to put in hard work, time, sweat, and sacrifice is welcome to be a Spartan. Robbie made the team but never played, not even in the blowouts and rarely at practice.

 One day in May, the pink flowers had blossomed on shrubs I passed on my walk to the library where I studied for final period. I sneezed terribly because of the pollen in the air and the returning green. The windows behind stacks of books looked into the courtyard dividing the main areas of the school from the athletic facility. I couldn't see anything, but I heard about it. Robbie was on his back as he lifted weights. Tommy came over, pressed the bar into Robbie's chest, and told him he needed more weight, otherwise he wasn't going to get stronger, practice more, or play in games like the rest of them. Robbie began to cough and squirm. Some of the other players stepped in to pull off Tommy but stopped and laughed. Robbie shot up from the bench, yelled at Tommy, and threw weights at him. Tommy yelled back and approached Robbie. The two yelled some more. Robbie grabbed some other weights and slammed them on the ground. Tommy told him to clean it up and added a vulgar word describing Robbie. They said Robbie cried at first before turning red and snatching Tommy by the throat. When Tommy couldn't push him away, Robbie hit him in the face with a dumbbell. The

OCTOBER

other teammates rushed over, but Robbie kept them away, scrapping with a few of them until the coaches intervened.

Running out of the facility and finding me in the library, he told me all about this. His face had been stripped of its youth, as though it had been left out in the rain and unprotected from a world with which he could have shared so much of himself, had he not seen it as turning against him every time he stepped into it. He ran to the parking lot and sped away in the Mustang his parents bought for his birthday. He had talked about using it to get out of Cole the first chance he could. I rode in it a few times to grab lunch or for a ride home. I offered money for gas every time, but he never took it. We listened to the music our parents said we couldn't listen to or buy until we had jobs. He let me smoke cigarettes, as long as the widows were down and I held my head and hand out the door. I made sure he drove the long way home to my house, using the county roads where people who knew me wouldn't be out at that time of day. If they had been on those backroads, they would have heard two teenagers singing at the top of their lungs to jangly guitars and backbeats and would have smelled cheap tobacco smoke after we flew by. When he left school that day, I didn't know where he went, but I found out where he had been.

Dad pulled into our driveway late from work. He had a meeting about inventory he had to attend. It went longer than planned, and on his way home, he ran into traffic. Cop cars blocked the road leading to Benson Bridge. It was dusk, and Dad said they had wrapped someone in a blanket after helping him down from the ledge. A crowd of people formed, having emerged from the cars idling along the road. An ambulance pulled in on the other side. The cops eventually let traffic through, and on his way by, my dad got a good look at the young man.

"Robbie Schmidt Jr."

"What?" Mom covered her mouth.

"Robbie?" My stomach sank with my fork falling to the floor.

"He was there but didn't jump. Maybe the cops talked him out of it, or he came down on his own."

Mom wrapped her arms around me.

"Are you sure it was him?" I asked.

"Without a doubt. They put him in the ambulance and drove away."

Dad poured a whiskey and loosened his tie. He pushed around his dinner. Sipping from her water, Mom glanced at me. All the things I should have said to Robbie crawled up my throat, but I couldn't reach for my glass. I slid my plate away after juice from the roast had hollowed out the potatoes.

Dad reached for our hands, and I hesitated closing my eyes to what was coming but squeezed them as tight as I could because I did not want to see the river or bridge or the place Robbie had reached after he left school and where I could have followed him

OCTOBER

rather than coming home. Dad asked God to help and be with Robbie and his family. We prayed for Tommy and young men like him and for young men like Robbie. We prayed for the school and gave thanks because nothing went further than Robbie standing on a stone-and-wood ledge overlooking the highest and rockiest point of the Chickataw where, on any ordinary day, traffic would slow down because of men fishing or people stopping in the middle of the bridge to see how far the water flowed, especially in spring, after the snow melted, until the river disappeared inside the light it reflected and the rows of flowers it flowed between.

Everyone stared at me the next day at school. It wasn't a cruel stare, but they looked at me as though I could hand over all the gears inside Robbie and put them in correct order.

Katie Shelby grabbed my arm. "Were you with him? Paul Simms said you were. He said he drove past Benson Bridge and saw your dad waiting."

I shook my head no and continued to class where the whispers paused after the teacher called us to order.

And before I realized it, the last month of school ended. My time as an adolescent was over. I wasn't ready for more classes. I decided not to go to college and, instead, find a job, which was as a typist for Heath and Stroh Public Accountants before Mr. Stroh recommended me to the Department of Public Works and Utilities, which took to me Early Bird, which opened the door to my position at the downtown branch of Cole Public Library where I eventually met Ray and, from time to time, saw classmates come in when they were single, married, divorced, with and without children, making ends meet, or struggling. We knew each other, made small talk, were polite. I made enough money to eventually move out of my parents' place. My first apartment was close enough, if I needed them, which I tried not to. Around this time, I stopped going to church. My parents weren't happy with my decision, but I needed a break, which was mostly true. That break turned into a long absence until I met Ray.

    Robbie never attended graduation. I don't know if he graduated at all—if, after things cleared up, he was allowed to. Tommy graduated and went on to play football at a good program until he blew out his knee in the Sugar Bowl. He runs a business supplying airplane parts and is a grandfather. Robbie's name was listed on the program, but it must have been there out of dignity. He disappeared. I was never able to talk to him. He never reached out to me, and as much as I wanted to reach out to him, I didn't.

    During my thirtieth high-school reunion, my phone rang quite a bit, and the caller on the other end would not leave a message on the answering machine, or the phone would click quiet before I could answer. Some of my classmates said Robbie married a teacher from New York, where they lived for a while

OCTOBER

before settling down in Vernon near his parents, who moved east of there, near the state line, not long after graduation. I heard he has two children and a small farm with horses, pigs, and a big pond. Dad said he thought he saw Mr. Schmidt between Cole and Vernon. Mom said Mrs. Schmidt corresponded only by mail or at her house. The press eventually left them alone. These are rumors, but I like hearing those rumors because they tell me Robbie is in a better place, but at other times, I want to meet the person behind those rumors and see and hear him until his flesh-and-blood life steps out of the shadows of the words someone else said about him.

• • •

Evening darkens more as I lounge in my car before heading home. My legs are tired, my ankles swollen, my fingers chilled and aching, but all that pain revives me, proves I am alive and moved through a few more hours of the day in a place I can, and have to, get to. I drink a little water and toast myself for doing this without needing any help and most certainly without the county calling in Search and Rescue because I got lost or slipped off a ledge—or did but still dusted myself off and found my way back into town like some wild white-haired woman from the woods covered in fall colors, twigs, and animal hides and bones, meandering in the streets like a flood. That would sure give Cole something to talk about over coffee and in church. I'll wake up tomorrow a bit stiff. Maybe I'll be back up to snuff by the time Halloween gets here. But I'll know I walked farther into the woods than I ever had, at least since Ray died. My old turnaround point became a new point, and every section of the trail afterward also became new. I did not look at my watch, but at one point, I stopped for what must have been for a few seconds, but it felt longer, as a moment like that often feels when you move from day into night and fall's gray-yellow, like a film over light, hangs around you, and you want to say something to it before everything turns bare when you're out here again, but you can't—still can't after all these years—but you realize not saying anything at all and simply showing up is as good as, if not better than, wondering if you said the right thing or would have another chance to speak again. I added to my steps, and I did not worry about hunger or thirst. I placed one foot in front of the other. Stones on my walk were like the stones in Saul's photo and all those rocks surrounding the lake behind the cabin in the mountains when Ray and I were there.

As I walked Big Oaks trail, the sun burned itself between tree trunks and the scrap of blue horizon and sunk more as evening approached, but I had my jacket and could not stop where I usually stopped. I did not know where, or if, the trail ended. I had no other plan other than to keep moving and to reach some point of the river where I could walk through the convergence of water, land, and the changing season. My last few moments in the

OCTOBER

woods appeared like small lanterns used for telling travelers in the old days where they were, where they could go, and where they had been.

More leaves will fall when I am not here, but I will see them and walk through them when I return. The river will flow with or without me seeing, hearing, or walking alongside it. When November's temperatures and winter overtake this fall weather, I will, weather permitting, walk out here in frost, patches of snow, and inside the bare trees looking like frames of stained-glass windows when the sky shines behind them.

I stopped where I stopped—day ending and night dampening the path. It was time to go back, and so, hastened by growing shadows and the last scraps of light, I walked back to the parking lot. I went a long way out in order to come back in. I didn't want to go anywhere else with anything alongside me, other than what I brought with me. Ray would still be gone, I would still have Saul's photo and his promise but no Saul, and the silence of the preserve will be very much like the silence at my house. And yet if I go past today's turnaround point, I could make it all the way to the county line, which is invisible but defined and where I could take myself no farther.

7

Late Saturday morning there's a knock on my door, and when I open it, Davis, avoiding me, spins in place and motions to Karen, who appears from around the corner, wearing her favorite denim dress and high-top sneakers, much higher, thicker-soled, and brighter than his. She holds a covered tray. Davis is dressed in his khakis and a green polo shirt tightening across his belly. His hair is gelled back, the longer parts of it feathering over his ears, and when my screen door opens all the way, pulling in the outside air, it's clear Davis has doused himself in cologne, but he does not have on his work boots, which, save for the cologne, means he's not headed to work today.

"Well, hello, you two. Come in, come in."

As they shuffle inside my apartment, I take a tray from Karen, pop its lid, and roll my lips into oohs after seeing the cupcakes. Plastic spiders, bats, skeletons, ghosts stick out from the orange and white frosting.

"They're yummy. I taste-tested to be sure."

"As the baker, you absolutely have to do that. Thank you. We're so close to Halloween, aren't we?"

"I can't believe it's next week," she says, smiling.

OCTOBER

Davis remains quiet and slides his hands in his pockets.

"What can I get y'all to drink?" I turn to the cabinets and grab plates and silverware.

"Tea, please." Karen sets out napkins for us before whispering, "*Davis.*" She nudges him with her shoulder.

"The usual," he mumbles. He looks away from us, especially me.

I reheat my coffee in the microwave and start water on the stovetop and drop a bag of chamomile for Karen into my Cole Cavaliers mug. I pour Davis his favorite—a tall glass of half-chocolate and half-white milk.

"What are you two up to today?" I ask, looking at both of them and stopping on Davis.

His eyes return to the counter, and he wipes his upper lip with his forearm.

"Not much. Errands and maybe clean the apartment." Karen unwraps three cupcakes and places them on the plates. "I want to go to the shelter, but Davis says it's definitely not time for a dog now."

"Are Mr. Weismann and Ginny going to let you have one?"

"We haven't talked to them. Davis was supposed to."

Davis grimaces behind his milk.

"You're not going to just bring one in, are you? I'd hate for them to take it away because they don't allow it or the lease says otherwise. I'm sure they'd be OK with it, but you better check first."

"We will."

"You've been talking about this for so long. Is today really the day?"

"No," Davis mutters.

"We'll see."

I peel off a cupcake's paper and smile at the gravestone in the frosting before pulling it out. "You don't want to rush into something important like that. Big responsibility." I stand up when the kettle whistles, and when I turn back to Davis and Karen, they are quieter than usual. Their eyes flit about. Davis looks around the kitchen and sighs when he stares out the screen door. He places his hands in his lap. His knees shake. He doesn't look at me much, and neither does Karen. They fumble holding their hands.

"We have to tell you something, Patty. We have news."

"More than a dog?"

"Yes." Karen turns somber.

Steam rises from the cup as I pour the hot water. I put a little honey in the bottom. Karen likes it that way.

"We're moving."

"Oh." I keep pouring. The hot water spills on the counter and drips onto the floor. "Did Wendy find a different place for you in town?"

OCTOBER

"No. Taylor."

"Taylor? When?"

"Before the end of the year."

"Well." Bracing myself on the counter, I wipe up the spilled hot water. My hands burn a little. I clear my throat. "Congratulations. The big city. How about that?" I stand up and pretend my coffee needs warming in the microwave.

"We got jobs at Davis's uncle's cafe. Wendy says we can do it. It would be good for us. She'll still check in on us, she said. She knows people there."

I hum and nod as I drink from my cold cup.

"We'll be helping him. Baristas. Baking."

"Like today."

"I'll make you a mocha when you come in."

"I'll have to do that, won't I? You better make me a good one, too." I reach for Karen's hands but end up tapping the counter between us. "That's really great. I'm so happy for you two." I smile at Davis who hasn't budged in his silence.

"We'll have to live with Davis's mom."

"But just for a little bit?"

"No." Karen shakes her head. "It's for good. She has a big house and said we can have the basement to ourselves. It's ready to go. Big TV. Internet. Big kitchen. It's bigger than here."

"That's not saying much, is it?" I stare out the front door. The daylight brightens the decorations in the yard. I clear my throat again. "Are we still set on the same scary music from last year?"

Karen nods, a little more excited. Davis's eyes drift to the walls.

"Our last one."

"Go big or go home, right?" I say, opening my eyes and smiling when after she says that.

"We'll miss you. You'll have to come visit."

"I certainly will. I have not been to Taylor in a long time."

"It's got a computer store and Uncle Marty's coffee shop, and there's a museum. Davis says it's tiny but mighty. They have a lot of art."

"I remember that museum. I haven't been there in a long time." My eyes move from Karen to Davis, who doesn't finish his milk.

After pushing his half-eaten cupcake toward the middle of the table, Davis slides off his stool and stuffs his hands in pockets. "They have all these trains," he mumbles.

"That's something new. I don't remember trains being there. Where do they go?"

"Everywhere. But we're too big."

"I could run it."

"They won't let you."

"We should have a hayride before y'all leave," I say. "A big Happy Halloween send-off for the last time."

OCTOBER

"That would be fun. I forgot my sweater. I'll see you out front." Karen kisses Davis on the cheek. "Bye and thank you, Patty. See you soon." She hugs me goodbye.

Davis starts for the door but turns halfway. "Miss Patty?"

"Hmm?"

"Thank you for everything while we lived here. I'll miss you."

I fumble again with the tray's plastic lid before handing it to him. "I'll miss you, too."

"I'll be sad not to see you, but we have to go."

"Yes, you do." I lift my Cole Cavaliers mug. "Taylor will be good."

He hugs me goodbye and leaves through my front door as quietly as he came in. The sky brightens, and today will be shorter than yesterday. Karen joins him out front, links her hand in his. They wave to me once more and walk down the small stone pathway between the road and our house. The regional bus arrives, hissing on its brakes, and its door opens before lowering down. Davis helps Karen in. The steps help Davis in.

· · ·

At least one bathroom stop waits for me on the highway between here and Taylor, which is notorious for being torn up, forced into one lane, cutting off access to the smaller towns along the way, and never finished. Most of the traffic I run into on my way out of Cole is folks headed to Sunday brunch or a

Sunday get-away to the big city. Before I left, I smashed two pieces of bread onto a mound of peanut butter and jelly and considered taking some carrot sticks but grabbed a handful of potato chips and one of Karen's cupcakes—the one with a black cat arching its back and its four paws deep in orange frosting. I tossed my sack lunch and coat in the passenger's seat. It was near nine-thirty when I hit the road. I didn't sit on the porch with my coffee and read the paper as I normally do on Sunday mornings, see Davis and Karen off on their way to church, or make plans with them for later in the day. The clouds stalled over Cole break up in my rearview mirror when the exit sign for the Taylor Art Museum and Historical Center arrives. The website said they are closed Mondays and Tuesdays, but they are open today until five. Before shutting down my computer, I checked email. Nothing other than reminders, bills, junk, and spam waited for me.

When I was young, my parents brought me here to an exhibition about modern art that stirred the locals. "Not Art as We Know It" the editorials cried. "Disgusting, Deviant, Devilish" and "Your Taxes Paid for This?" We brought Aunt June, Dad's middle sister. She aspired to be a painter, and she loved every piece hanging on the walls and sitting on a pedestal. Her works looked like fields with washed-out wildflowers, layers of them, seen from high above. Sometimes she used a hairbrush. Sometimes, Dad told me, she scraped paint with an old toothbrush and a hog bristle before Grandpa Dennis tossed it

OCTOBER

out. She painted her visions on large bolts of cloth that ended up at the back of the family barn, where, deeper in the back, she worked and hid her work under tarps. June Bug wrote words and phrases underneath the paint. "Poems," Dad said, after spying some when he stumbled upon them. "But they weren't clear enough to read. Maybe something about the journey of the soul. I'm not sure, but it looked like that's what she meant."

Aunt June never married, and after a man abruptly ended their relationship, never dated anyone as long as I knew her. She struggled with holding a regular job everyone expected her to hold because it was her only source of income, but Dad encouraged her to pursue the one thing not making her anxious, breaking her down into tears, or pressing its weight on her during the hours she was most awake and alone. That one time I came across one of her paintings I looked closely but could not find the words placed within her and she had placed in front of me—the words she never asked to hear but had heard anyway and knew she had to place somewhere.

A guard strolls toward the doors at the back of the lobby as he quiets his walkie-talkie. A large metal mobile spreads under the middle of the ceiling and over my path to the front desk. According to the panel on the wall, it's the museum's newest acquisition. With its neon colors and squiggly shapes, it looks like a giant bird a child created. The bio for the international artists said he died a long time ago after forging this one-of-a-kind piece available in the gift shop as replicas, in three sizes, I can purchase for a discount if I become a museum member today.

"Hello. Is this your first time here?" another guard asks, motioning to the bag and coat check.

"No, but it's been a long time."

"Welcome back."

"Thank you." I take the number for my coat and purse and pick up a floor map and exhibition guide. The main floor is devoted to the museum's permanent collection. The second floor has the special traveling exhibition. The trains Davis and Karen mentioned have their own annex.

Regional tribes, black folk, white folk, men, women, and children created or once owned most of the first floor's historical artifacts—paintings and sculptures, clothes, quilts, tools, letters, furniture. A vitrine holds tickets for a riverboat, a stage coach, a train (*The Tri-Valley Thunder*), and the Taylor Airport before International was added to its name decades later. On the next wall hangs an old hunting rifle with its accompanying advertisement—a man and his dog emerging from the woods and chasing a turkey. An ammunitions manufacturer set up its waterwheel for production near a tributary and remained in business for one hundred and fifty years.

Sunrise on the Chickataw is the room's main piece. Thomas Burns-Petit moved here from Illinois in the mid-1800s after hearing about "elysian fields, sparkling water, and a fiery sunset

OCTOBER

charging the land with God's redeeming, eternal presence." The large oil painting took him four years to finish. He fought off creditors, snobbery, alcoholism, depression, the deaths of his wife and daughters, the growth of industries in a natural setting, and mounting national and local tensions. A mob beat and shot him, at forty-five years of age, after he and a local preacher and his congregation argued over the interpretation of the Bible regarding slavery and the treatment of slaves by folks who called themselves Christian. In the painting, a bright green forest surrounds the river. One bird chases another bird in the sky and over the forest and water that drew Burns-Petit. Around a bend, where spring rains raised the water for a swift but dangerous escape, a canoe churns in the Chickataw and holds slaves and the abolitionists, cradling rifles, who freed and protected them from silhouettes lurking along the banks and among the trees and raising their rifles in the light of a new day.

 After several small rooms and halls, the first floor ends with a series of photographs by a contemporary artist. She was born and raised in the area, left, and returned to Boyetta, a town outside Taylor. Her studio used to be a warehouse. She has captured the times I know—dilapidated buildings, rusted vehicles, old signs, weeds choking out what had been crops, churches moving into strip malls, and anxieties and traumas, fears, and hopes. In each black-and-white photo, families of many skin colors smile, laugh, and in one particular piece, dance in a ring, holding hands, their heads tossed back, eyes up, under stars like white roses cast across dark water.

    Up the stairs I go to the special exhibition *One and Many*. After a three-month run, the show will end in December, and my pamphlet reminds me about the annual holiday auction and the Holiday Train "perfect for the young and the young at heart." Museum members can bring in their art for auction, the proceeds of which will to go a homeless shelter in town. A few patrons ahead of me talk somewhere in the room, but when I enter, they disappear as though they are ghosts.

    Most of the art—be it paper, canvas, or shaped in clay or stone—depicts a body or several bodies frozen in an activity. Wrestling, kissing, fighting. Teachers arguing with their students. A close-up shot of football teams striking as soon as the ball is snapped. An aerial shot of senators filling senate chambers. The opposite of the show's theme is alongside these works. The solitary people cast out of society, never accepted in the first place, or feigning acceptance but always knowing where they stand in relation to everyone. Sometimes they are happy, sometimes sad, but they are always present. The lone guitarist onstage. The office worker who walks the path between cubicles, her head looking down at a file in her hands, and her coworkers ignoring or gossiping about her. One Japanese silkscreen depicts a lone monk battling a giant dragon. The tail wraps around his waist, sword, and quiver of arrows. The label says the silkscreen

OCTOBER

is part of a training manual in which the warrior must become one with the obstacle inhibiting the way forward, even if that means moving back or side to side for the time being until the path reveals itself.

    A simple etching of St. Jerome in the wilderness, no bigger than a greeting card, stops me. The burly lion lies at his feet, once his enemy but now his companion after he removed the thorn from the lion's paw. The rocks and the trees of the arid climate rise around the saint and encircle him like crooked hands. He retreated to the desert to wipe clean his life, and he is not in want of anything material of this world and is not afraid of losing anything that is never his in the first place, not even his life. Next to him is a Bible and the stone he beats to his chest for repentance. It's neither day nor night in the etching. In the background stands a crucifix around which the light from the sky falls and finds a place to bind everything together.

    At the end of the special exhibition, I walk down a flight of stairs, turn a corner, walk outside, past the garden with mulch and the pond with ducks quacking at me, cross under the trellis, and stand outside the Daniel Stearns Train Gallery. When Davis and Karen said "trains," the iron horses of yesteryear, depots, and cabooses chugged through my head. But when I enter the gallery, streams of model trains—red, black, silver, classic, and modern—fly through miniature landscapes filled with plastic people, trees, cars, buildings, and scenes for their backdrops.

WILLIAM AUTEN

    I start at winter. Each electric engine pulls passenger cars, lumber, or airplane parts between blankets of cotton, banked like snow, and wintry woodlands and over bridges, above jelly-like rivers and frozen lakes, stops under the towns' ice-crusted roofs, or slows down near the ski resort where people ice fish in front of a giant wall of puffy white clouds and painted snowflakes frozen in the gray sky. Fireplaces glow inside houses. Smoke wafts from chimneys. Kids build snowmen and forts. Santa and his reindeer jangle in the sky behind us. Near a front section of this scene, a car has spun off the road. The family and their dog wait knee-deep in the snow. A tow truck is on its way. When some trains in this scene blow their whistles, the tow truck bobs its crane and flashes the lights on its roof.

    Tiny plastic flowers bloom in spring. Miniature trees are green. People slowly appear from their hovels and blankets. A school bus opens its doors to children waiting on a neighborhood corner. Dressed in shorts and raincoats, they hold umbrellas, ball gloves, lunchboxes, and books. A group of girls jumps rope. A river cuts through the crowded town square welcoming anyone from anywhere.

    One train through summer takes its time at the drive-in movie theater playing an old cartoon on the tiny screen, while another train slows down near the baseball stadium, which, when the trains arrives, brightens with cheering fans, a flashing scoreboard, and floodlights no bigger than quarters. A bat hitting

OCTOBER

a baseball cracks through speakers on a nearby metal post. The crowd roars when the little batter shimmies in the box.

And then, fall is revealed as a circus scene. The plastic trees the model trains zigzag through have turned orange, red, and yellow, some of them are bare, and some of the fake leaves scatter on the paths between the big red-and-white tent, the toy animals, the replica of a midway with blinking rides and screams and laughter coming from speakers under the diorama's tables. The crowds are motionless as though in a dream they wait for the Ferris wheel, bumper cars, food shacks, the roller coaster zipping under my chin, and rows of miniature posters promising AMAZEMENT, THRILLS, AND ODDITIES for the sideshows within.

Next to the exit doors is a donation box with a printed note. Dr. Warner B. Stearns, a retired surgeon from New York City, is now a philanthropist fulfilling his love of art and history. He met his wife Nancy when she danced on Broadway. Trains fascinated the doctor when he was young, and he collected as many of them as he could, and when he retired, the Taylor Art Museum and Historical Center accepted his donation of behalf of the town's long history of trains. The gallery is named after the couple's son. While the Stearnses' daughter went on to become a veterinarian, the son, Danny, died from childhood leukemia. The money goes to a research fund Dr. Stearns and some of his colleagues established. The Stearnses decorated Danny's room with all things related to trains, most of which had been Dr. Stearns's when he was that age. They want us to know the trains belonging to Danny belong to everyone who, before moving on, stopped here to watch them pass through the seasons.

・・・

Signs for the Taylor Fair and Miss Ledbetter's Haunted Hayride and Pumpkin Patch Maze glow in my headlights on my way back home. Admission to both venues is called the Double, and they are connected in more ways than one. Generations of families run deep in both places—as guests and as employees. Jessie Ledbetter's grandchildren run the farm and own the land the fair uses. I've known a few folks seasonally employed there for this time of year when the fairgrounds and Miss Ledbetter's transform from autumn haunts to Thanksgiving comfort foods and drinks and then to all things Christmas and wintertime. For years, Davis, Karen, and I have talked about doing the Double and making a big day of it all, especially after getting the house ready for Halloween. Another billboard reminds me how much SCARY FALL FUN awaits me ONLY FIVE MINUTES AWAY —FOOD, THRILLS, GAMES, SIDESHOWS. Taking the exit would add more time to my drive, but stopping there on a whim would not be my first time.

The man who sat next to me in the surgery waiting room flipped through the TV when his show went to break. I couldn't

OCTOBER

read my book and didn't want to skim through the magazines because I had skimmed them during Ray's first bout with cancer. A commercial for the Taylor Fair flickered on the screen.

"That is loads of fun. We always have a good time with the kids," the man said, pointing with the remote while we waited to be called back by a doctor.

The talk show came back on, and the guests cried and yelled through love, abandonment, and who wanted to be with whom—couples, adopted children, old flames not seen in years. The man next to me sniffled and wiped his eyes. The sun had set then, too. That hospital had cooped me up for hours.

"I'm going for dinner. I need something other than the cafeteria," I said to the nurse on duty, who nodded and returned to his computer.

<But I didn't get food. I drove to the fair. I just up and left. I lied to him.>

<I don't think that nurse cared.>

<No, I lied to Ray. I left him there.>

<You didn't. It makes sense. You had to breathe. It was OK to want that. And God when Courtney was laid up in the hospital with her cancer the first thing I wanted was a cold beer from our fridge at home. I would've paid anyone any amount to get that for me, but I would've rather done it myself to get out there and get out of my head.>

\<Stepping into that world relieved me of everything waiting for me when I got back. Afterward I felt so guilty.\>

\<Stepping away was not selfish. And feeling guilty is understandable. You came back. Besides where was any of that going to go? Ray's condition wasn't going to go anywhere. The nurse would treat him like any other patient there. Not favoritism or lack thereof but part of the job.\>

\<I know but still.\>

\<You find a way through it. Or it finds a way for you.\>

From the hospital, I bypassed one of my favorite burger joints. I was hungry, but I didn't want to eat. I drove down Allston Street, turning right onto Highway 17, and out toward Suffolk Springs, where on one side of the land, in the coming night, Taylor Fair blared, rides rumbled, and a spectrum of lights blinked and swirled. Directly across from it, divided by turnstiles and ticket booths, lay Miss Ledbetter's with its lines snaking in and out from the front and into the haystacks and flatbeds pulled by tractors.

My ticket that night was only for entry into the fair. For rides, additional tickets had to be purchased. But I didn't want to ride anything. Most of them violently whipped you around, up and down, forward and backward. The chances were pretty good I would sit next to someone I knew, but I wanted to be by myself and recognized by no one. No additional tickets were needed for

OCTOBER

the exhibitions or, lining the midway with all their screams, laughs, and lights, the sideshows.

I started in the science building and passed plenty of booths and demonstrations, including one of the sixth-grade classes experimenting with magnets and motion and how the two work together by pulling in one thing at a time until many things accumulated into a larger thing not capable of changing without an opposite external force. They observed things with mass in motion started with the small, first thing.

Entrepreneurs and government officials wanted my contact information or wanted to give me stats and data about projects, such as the proposed high-speed train between Taylor and DeMint, stopping along the way at the little dot representing Cole. The project would have to negotiate the Chickataw River Preserve. A gentleman next to me voiced his opinion of the sprawling woodlands and river life that would be disturbed, to which the gentlewoman behind the table encouraged him to "continue having this conversation." The estimated budget had several zeroes, and the estimated completion date seemed too near. "I'll believe it when I see it," I told them before moving on to the Animal Husbandry Building taking me back to growing up with farmers in the family. I petted my share of donkeys, goats, and horses. I lost fake money on a gerbil race when, rather than scampering around the course, my guy Mr. Buttercup chewed on his food pellets and mounted Lilly next him, which brought on giggles, blushing, and, from some parents, covering their children's eyes.

My last stop before the midway was the Sights and Sounds of Outer Space, chock full of interactive panels and a simulated trip to the discovery of a planet inhabitable for humans. Before it was over and we all exited through a portable gift shop, the voiceover asked if we are alone in the universe and concluded not knowing so much is better than knowing so many things that aren't so.

A man dressed in a lab coat shouted at us cruising the midway, divided by food vendors and games of skill and chance on one side and, on the other, sideshows of strength, wonder, and oddities—including his. A young woman stood next to him. Half of the yellow font on the poster behind them was normal. The other half was frenzied like the red font for a horror movie. A lightning bolt divided the middle, where on one side stood a young woman with her eyes closed and on the other side raged a gorilla.

The girl next to the scientist wore pigtails and a simple dress. Had she not been part of the show, I wouldn't have noticed her, or I would have assumed she belonged to those of us in the crowd because she was so very plain. She curtsied when we circled around the entry into the tent. Dr. Mandrake, "*the* Dr. Theodore Mandrake," theatrical with his thick English accent, said we would be witness to an act of unprecedented change and a firsthand insight into the human condition. "Are we as civilized

OCTOBER

as we pride ourselves in being? Do we appeal to the better angels of our natures? Or do our beastly natures remain within…and can return?" Smiling at her, he turned to the girl who invited us in with her spreading arms. "She will become who she truly is."

People packed the tent. I found one of the last seats at the back. Kids started to cry even before the show started. A few parents excused themselves with children whimpering on their way out. A makeshift science lab hummed on stage. Beakers and tubes. Stacks of papers on a desk. Several diplomas and equations on the walls. A blackboard with more equations and scribbled handwriting. And in the left corner, a giant matte-black box tall enough for someone to walk into and wide enough for someone, or something, to walk out of.

The music overhead stopped. The audience lights went dark, and the stage lights dimmed. Dr. Mandrake strutted out, adjusted a few things on the desk, and double-checked the blackboard. Welcoming us, he reintroduced himself and mentioned at least four degrees and the ability to speak many current and dead languages. His hands dramatically tugged his lab coat before fanning the air. He was very confident in the process we were about to experience and his role in it. He assured us every precaution had been set in place—nothing in the experiment would go awry.

"Is it progress, or is it regress? Forward or backward? Either way, it is the transformation of life itself! Motion made memorial!"

He called for his daughter, and the young woman in pigtails and the plain dress who stood outside the tent entered offstage. Daisy curtsied to us and sat in the chair. Dr. Mandrake explained the process a little more. He poured a dark-purple potion, handed the glass to her. After Daisy drank, she stepped into the black box. Before she did, they said, "I love you" to each other as calmly as two people knowing they would see each other again in the future. When he asked her if she was afraid of what could happen, she replied she was not.

Once inside, the heavy door closed and sealed with a bolt tightening and a hissing sound. Everyone in the crowd grew quiet. Not even the sounds of the midway and the rest of the fair outside the tent seeped in. The light shining above Daisy's head glowed brighter. Her face was clear and smooth like an angel's. Her father spoke, and hypnotized by the chemical in her, she closed her eyes while standing there. Her father asked the "real Daisy" to come forth. The young woman shivered. The light above her faded, and as it did, an image appeared, and I couldn't tell if the gorilla had been inside the box with her or had stepped in front of her, somehow letting her shine through like a ghost covering the person it emerged from.

OCTOBER

Daisy slowly faded away until only the gorilla remained. Dr. Mandrake commanded the animal inside to remain calm.

"Daisy, my lovely daughter, my child," he soothed.

Her eyes narrowed, her nose wrinkled, and her large teeth bared. And as quickly as her temperament intensified, she subsided. Silence and tension electrified the tent. Dr. Mandrake drifted away from the black box, turned to us, and bowed. We started to clap, and his face whitened.

"Stop! Please, no noise!" His index finger thrust over his lips.

The gorilla's eyes popped wide, canines flaring.

The black box's door burst open. The gorilla huffed, snarled, and threw objects, smashed glass and broke things. She jumped into the audience, thundering up and down the aisles, terrifying and exhilarating everyone, especially the kids who laughed and cried like the adults. She stopped alongside me and loomed like a heavy, hot shadow that would leave if I opened my eyes and told her I was afraid but am no longer.

Dr. Mandrake corralled her back into the box and transformed her into the young woman she started as but not without nearly losing his life.

I glanced at the person sitting next to me. Our mouths were agape, and we wiped tears from our eyes. We patted our chests. Sweat dampened my back and underarms like it was summer and not October.

Laughing and crying, the crowd broke up, but I sat there by myself at the back catching my breath. I could not move. The audience lights returned to normal, and the overhead music clicked on. The young actress, make-up removed, a robe covering her dress, peeked through the curtain off to the side from where she had stepped onto stage.

Although something different had changed inside her, she stood there as plainly as she had before she changed and would plainly stand there for the next show, the remainder of that night, and into tomorrow. She disappeared behind the curtain and into the fair's sights and sounds. And after sitting a few more seconds, I left, but I also wanted to linger and believe for a little longer in what had unfolded in front of me, even if it was all an illusion.

Before I returned to the hospital, I stopped at Fast Lane and ate my fried-chicken sandwich and fries and drank my strawberry malt. I left an extra tip for the guys and gals working late.

Back at the hospital, the man who sat next to me had left, and a different nurse welcomed me into Ray's room. He was half-awake. The machines monitoring him beeped at a stable pace. I kissed his forehead and pulled the chair alongside his bed. A silence, different than the last time we were in a hospital after his surgery, tightened around us. I kept an eye on Ray and an eye on the door in case I had to fling it open if anything worsened. A coldness crawled across the room. I double-checked the window. The TV station blacked out for the end of the day, and the screen

OCTOBER

hovering over us like a box held our reflection. Neither Ray nor I moved, and nothing visible or invisible in that dark mirror moved or came for us.

* * *

Behind me, a long line of cars waits to enter the parking lots at the Taylor Fair and Miss Ledbetter's. Night is fully here, the temperature has dropped, and the crowds keep growing. Several food trucks stand outside the gates. Hot cocoa, popcorn, and coffee waft in through my car's heater.

The attendant at the ticket booth takes my money and sends me toward the line for the fair's main entrance. Most of the rides look the same as they did all those years ago, but some look new. The exhibition buildings have not changed location. Anything having to do with technology is mentioned far more than animals or nature, and most of them promise a "better future" or "improving lives one at a time" or aim to customize experiences as common as dirt and don't need any tinkering at all. Most of the sideshows seem tamer, but a few retain their appeal and promise of mystery. None of the attractions' list mentions anything about a show involving a girl transforming into a gorilla.

A group of teenagers buzz behind me. One of the girls has a streak of pink hair and several piercings along her ears sparkling in the lights.

Turning around, I say, "Would y'all like this? I know it's just one ticket, but."

The teens peer into my hand.

Nodding yes and taking it, the girl with pink hair says, "Thank you."

"We can buy more," says another girl adjusting her stocking cap.

The boys with them nod, their arms cradling fried foods and Cokes and the arms of their dates. No one in their group stands alone.

"Have fun," I reply, slipping out of line and walking to the parking lot.

I start my car and head back to Cole with at least another hour of driving. The ticket I bought was only for the fair, like before, not the Double, which is a promise between Davis, Karen, and me I intend to keep.

8

And then, from out of nowhere, Halloween arrives. The house is quiet so far at sunset. Davis and Karen must be napping, or they're finishing getting ready. I lay out my Bride of Frankenstein wig, with the two squiggles of lightning bolts in that mass of hair, and an old white bed sheet. For added drama, I'll slap on some pale makeup and black lipstick.

My costume my first year at the house was nothing more than a bandit's mask and my tattered and stained gardening gloves. I bought a toy cap gun and play money, stuffing the latter in a laundry bag Ray and I used to lug our dirty clothes down to the basement at the old house. Davis said he would arrest me if I caused any trouble. "But you're a teddy bear," I said, smiling at his costume matching Karen's. He didn't like that much, mainly because the teddy bears were Karen's idea, and Davis's wanted them to dress up as characters from one of his favorite movies of all time—Karen a Ghostbuster and he the Stay Puft Marshmallow Man. His other idea, which I saw in a page torn from his notebook, was for him to be a tornado and for Karen to be a meteorologist holding a weather map and a pointer, her hair pushed in all directions. "You or Patty can make this," he said, pulling from his pocket instructions he found on the Internet for sewing together several black and gray pillows until they formed a twister. Karen and I wondered where he would breathe beneath all that fabric. "You could die. Then where would I be?" Karen said before showing him a couple dressed like cute teddy bears. He shrugged his shoulders in agreement before kissing her.

Last year, I was a puppy dog with one spot around my eye, a red collar around my neck, and a rolled-up newspaper I painted brown with black and white spots and stuffed in my belt on my backside for a tail. I found treats both humans and dogs can eat, but they tasted like cookies left out too long in the sun. Another year, I was the Wicked Witch, Karen was Dorothy, and Davis was the Tin Man—he refused to be the Lion or the Scarecrow. "I'm not a coward or dumb," he let us know several times, and to which we agreed, but we teased him about dressing up as Toto. Being Oz crossed my mind. What fun to pretend to be great and powerful, a ruler over everything visible and invisible, but then to be humbled into revealing your small and exaggerated true self standing alone.

I unfold my Cole Cavaliers chair and plop down next to Stubbs. "Want anything to eat or drink before the trick-or-treaters show up? We don't want you dehydrated. You need to put on your best show tonight especially because this is the last hurrah here. The peach tea from Far + Away really is all that. And their pecan pie is *to die for*."

OCTOBER

My skeletal friend doesn't smirk at my joke. He has the same bone-dry look on his face he's had all the years we've set him out here. His eye sockets stare where the mesh of autumn tree leaves and the sky darkens the space in front of us.

"Suit yourself."

A stream of dark shapes flicker down the street. One butterfly. And then another one. And soon, several scamper in the air on their way south for the change of season. Behind their black-and-orange wings, walk shadows, some of which are no bigger than children, and those same shadows giggle and bump buckets or bags against their legs as they make their way from the hills of Cole to the doors of houses in the neighborhoods. I bet some of them will head over to downtown's parade or to Higher Grounds Church after their first pass for candy down here, and maybe, if Davis, Karen, and I are lucky, some of the crowds from those other destinations will make their way to the neighborhoods and our place for more sugar and good-natured scares. Stores will stay open late tonight, and the area will be chock full of costumes, kids, families, city and business leaders, and high school athletes, cheerleaders, and the band lining up and marching down Main Street until it bends into the sunset. Adult shadows will guide children shadows, some holding hands, as the route of the dead and the living will line up at the north end of Ashbery Street, the main drag in front of the house, down Pottawee, where the Sweet Briar neighborhood begins, and from there, they will scatter onto the various streets and cul-de-sacs and eventually make their way back onto Cornell Lane, chasing it until it intersects Ashbery where I and Davis and Karen will be dressed and waiting on our front porch or listening from inside the house for the voices coming closer. And like the butterflies unrolling in front of me like film, the shadows of the living and the dead need no direction. They go where they know to go.

As soon as the shadows' voices fade, one by one, the butterflies' path breaks up, and they sway down to the ground, and for a moment, the wings, so unified, drop like a veil. The butterflies leave, and in their place, darkness spreads from the edges of town and across the horizon and the many silhouettes.

The front garden holds the remains of summer flowers. Six months from now, it will bloom again. But for now, the garden retreats into cold wet dirt, withering green stalks, and bursts of warm colors. The first frost is on its way.

I have sat here so many times and, as Mom and Grandma Paris said, watched the world go by. Some days, after I finished gardening here at the house, or not even gardening that day, I cross-stitched with my basket full of needles and colors like a rainbow by my ankles. I stitched while rocking in the chair currently occupied by dear Stubbs. A wind would kick up and turn over the instructions I worked from—words or a scene, like a cabin by a stream, or, like I did for Ray's family one Christmas, the names of immediate family members and some great-greats

OCTOBER

going back several generations that took me several weeks to complete because the family tree was so intricate. The names were no bigger than the wings of a small butterfly. You had to get close to them to see the names and birth and death dates. The death dates of the names on the lower branches, closer to the present time, had yet to be filled in. But they were all there. I embroidered every one of them. I knew the world went by on human, animal, and insect wheels and legs—even the days and the weather come on their own legs. How else would everything get here? How else would everything end up untying before tying here in front of me then as now?

 Ray's shirts and slacks always required fixes at the last minute before he went to work. Missing buttons. Tears in sleeves or cuffs. His pants' pocket once caught the corner of his desk. His car keys and Chapstick dropped out. The gash practically converted his pants into shorts on one side. He looked like a man halfway to the beach for a much-needed vacation. We had a good laugh about Blue Sky's HR raising an eyebrow at his wardrobe that day.

 I started a stocking cap for Saul for Christmas. He could wear it while driving his convertible muscle cars. He told me his car's heater had been acting up. He could be warm inside while ignoring speed limits to reach his destination. But the stocking cap rests like a half-formed Easter egg in the small closet in my bedroom, lying atop other pieces I never finished, including a bib for Ginny and Mike's firstborn who came into this world when Ray's absence overwhelmed me.

<Red is my favorite color.>

<OK. Thanks for telling me. I have plenty of red.>

<An all red stocking cap will be sharp on my bald head. Can you stitch 43 in there?>

<Where? On the front?>

<Wherever anywhere just so it's seen.>

<Sure. What color would you like for the numbers?>

<White.>

I waited a few seconds before typing <Why 43?>

<My old high school football number.>

<You played football?!>

<I sure did. Now I never said I was good at it. God can't hand out all the athlete genes to everybody everywhere. I rode the pine most of the time but it was fun to get in there when I could.>

<Any stories from your glory days?>

<Best game of my life was the one I played in at the very last minute. We were getting our butts handed to us by Adair and Coach sent all us scrubs in. The bench was cleared! Donny my best friend and me stared at each other. We were confused and excited at the same time. Donny may have even peed his pants from all the excitement. I made one tackle. Just one. But my dad saw me do it and it meant the world. It wasn't a highlight or

OCTOBER

anything but it was mine and his. Ours.> His cursor paused for a few seconds. <I take that back. It was all his. It wasn't mine. It was Dad's. That tackle was Dad's.>

<Why?>

<He and I never had a good relationship. He was always on me and my brothers to do this or that be this or that and by the time we did it it was too late in his eyes. Never good enough I guess but I know he meant well. He came from a rough upbringing. Tough SOB. He thought he was doing us a solid by the same. He was never that way with Lucinda and Marcy. They were Daddy's Girls and they milked it for all they could. But that one night I felt like I did him right. He even bought me a beer after the game. It was his way of saying he loved me.>

<One day out of the whole year.>

<What do you mean?>

<All it takes sometimes is one day out of the whole year to see everything through.>

<That's a good one PATRICIA.>

We said our goodnights, and I wrapped myself in Ray's old sweater until the computer shut down on the photo of me and him at the cabin and its last glow cast itself on his cane sitting in the corner by the desk.

That sweater I took to him when he was in the hospital in Cole after he coughed up blood, but he couldn't wear it because of his position in bed. The room was so cold, and Ray's body was so warm. The nurse let me lay it on him.

"Are you Sonny and Laura's daughter?" I asked her.

"Yes, ma'am, I am." She checked the machines behind Ray.

Her dad held a home-brewing tasting party one summer. We were new to the neighborhood, and Sonny and Laura welcomed us. Hawaii was the theme, and we all showed up in floral-print shirts and skirts. Ray and I had such a bad bout of gas later that night. Sonny's beer had clogged up everyone there. Our hands covered our stomachs as we mimed unpleasant sounds and smells. I told Gloria about it, and she said she and Bill went to Mexico for their wedding anniversary and a combination of green salsa and tequila did the same thing to her. "Avoid the green sauce. I'm telling you, girl," she warned me, laughing until she cried.

The adolescent Michelle had leis for us when we entered the back yard. She placed Ray's lei over his head as gently as she readjusted his sweater after I had laid it on him in his hospital bed. At the party, he was taller, but she was taller standing next to the IV tubes and taking his vitals. And in that hospital bed, with the sweater draped over him, was Ray, this grown man, shrinking from the inside, tubes jutting from his body, no one quite sure what was going on until the tests returned, and covered with a bright maroon sweater with some black and yellow accents

OCTOBER

around his once-chubby tummy. I wished I had finished my matching sweater.

The porch creaks under my chair when I stand up. My old body groans. Stubbs is not going anywhere. Someday I'll be like him. The procession keeps up around us. The dead talk to me and show me where they are and were as much as the living do. If I could take them all in, I would, not inside the house but inside me—nothing and no one left out. When this day is done, they will change out of their masks and slip into bed, ready for tomorrow, which will be as regular as the hours they waited to walk in—one evening reserved to be something or someone other than who they are.

Between the sunset and the moonrise, the future stands not too far away. The future is close but never really here. The present is like the mouth of a cave lit up at the front and darkened in the back. The past never announces itself, is always around, but not always seen. You could drop a rock in that cave and never hear it land. Only echoes would return.

But these dead in front of me are not masks or costumes. They are real, and they speak so much about being alive without flesh and without saying anything to me. The dead line up, one by one, and do not have to announce who they are.

A wave of children and their parents make their way to our end of the street and head this way. It's time. Makeup, wig, fill the bowls of candy, check in with Davis and Karen. I have to get ready for when the dead and the living knock on my door.

• • •

According to Davis's notebook, we have more trick-or-treaters than last year. Not much candy is left. The kids who came earlier in the night got more sweets than the later kids, which was a blessing because neither Karen nor I want any leftovers this year. Davis pockets one block of caramel and one package of hard fruit candy. I grab a handful. Karen doesn't take any. When he's loaded with sugar, Davis is like a puppy. We've tried buying fewer bags, which ran out faster and made us unpopular with the trick-or-treaters. We've bought candy we assumed Davis would not touch, which proved false. And we've thrown away unopened bags, which wasn't a smart financial decision. Our option this year was to let the early waves of kids take one of each, and as the night wore on, let the last groups take as much as they wanted.

Davis's index finger pulses over the large streaks of red pencil marks crossing the paper's blue lines. He and I count exactly twenty-two ticks. At the bottom, under a heavily scribbled horizontal line, he noted the costumes, especially repetitions ("Copycats," he snickers), and any neighbors we recognized, such as Dr. Grant and his two girls dressed respectively as a gladiator and a veterinarian—the former wielding a cardboard sword and

OCTOBER

shield and robed in a crimson t-shirt and armored in tin foil and the latter with a stethoscope placed on a toy horse. Davis cowered behind me when he realized his dentist stood on the front porch. Eight months ago, I took him to his last check-up and cleaning. He was due for another one but has been avoiding it and the calls from Adult Services, which I knew about because Wendy asked for help. Before Dr. Grant pivoted on the porch holding his girls' hands, he grabbed a lollipop from our candy bowl, unwrapped it, and winked at Davis while popping his thumb over his finger-gun.

"Neck still bothering you?" I ask Davis as he closes his notebook.

"Yes," he says, digging his fingers under his lace collar and into his skin turning as red as a strawberry.

"That's what you get. Dr. Grant will tell you the same thing. Miss Wendy will too," Karen says, bringing in the last bowl from the porch.

"He fixes teeth. He's not that other kind of doctor. Same thing with Wendy. She helps us downtown. She's not a dentist."

I head for the medicine cabinet in my bathroom and return with a bottle of calamine lotion and cotton swabs. "You let that dry, and come back tomorrow for more, if you need it. OK?"

"Thank you, Patty." He removes his red wig, opens a carton of chocolate milk from my fridge, and flops in the chair next to Stubbs.

Karen kisses him on his cheek and holds his hand as she stands next to him. The moon and the front porch's light frame them looking toward the street, the shadows moving up and down, in and out of the neighborhood, and the voices laughing and screaming. Their red-and-white-striped socks line up, and Davis' denim overalls contrast the white apron covering Karen's light-blue shirt. They hug each other. For a brief moment, holding each because of love and the holiday, not out of fear, they spot-on resemble Raggedy Ann and Andy. I tell myself to hold onto that image for next year, when they will not be on this porch handing out candy and being just-enough scary with me.

"We'll see you in the morning to help clean up, Patty," Karen says. "This was fun. Happy Halloween."

"It sure was. See y'all tomorrow. Good night. Davis?"

He pivots.

"You keep first watch for ghosts and demons and all the things that will go bump in the night. We're all counting on you."

His grin is so huge and serious before he leaves.

They hug me goodnight and head toward their half of the house.

"Happy Halloween."

As soon as they leave, silence fills the space and pulls in neither sadness nor happiness but more like a place to wait between. The mirror along the wall between the front door and the little hallway to my bedroom snaps up my image wearing the

OCTOBER

black wig, black lipstick, and pale face and nearly scares me to death. A phantasmic, strange woman walks alongside me and follows me to my desk and the computer, as though the mirror is an open door to where she lives. I back up, nearly tripping on my long white dress, and the woman in the mirror nearly trips when she backs away from me. We stare at each other and tilt our heads one way. The weight of the massive beehive of hair stretches our necks to the floor. We lift our hands, pale with makeup, fingernails painted black. I wave. She waves. Our smiles are opposites. The scar on my left lip is on her right lip. A horse at Carmichael's farm gave it to me when I was young. A sudden spring storm surged over the field, lighting zipping in the distance, and scared him. He bucked me to the ground, where I landed cheek first on rocks sticking up through the grass. Dad, ahead of us on his horse, reached me and cradled my head in his lap, wiping my tears until Mrs. Carmichael arrived with a first-aid kit. Mr. Carmichael held the reins of four skittish horses like a puppet master pulling strings tied across the horizon. The ghostly makeup the woman in the mirror wears doesn't conceal her scar but highlights it like a mound of old snow packed on top with fresh snow. She emerges from the bright gray background with it, and she turns toward the edge of her mirror-door when I turn toward the kitchen, and floating away, she disappears between the glass and the wall as though she rides an animal deeper into her world.

WILLIAM AUTEN

My wrinkled face appears from behind my makeup and costume when I peel them off, and like an inevitable shadow, gravity follows quickly behind, pulling down and sagging my cheeks, jowls, and throat I had seen in other folks' faces when I was younger and didn't give a hoot something like that would ever happen to me. I flop my Bride of Frankenstein wig on the desk. The white squiggles in the mass of black hair are as white as my own shock of hair.

I pour myself a glass of ginger ale on ice and open a box of chocolate-chip cookies. Sherry Lynn gave me two nights off in a row while she worked a quick job at the rendering plant. She mentioned the smell could drive you insane, far more than the chemicals we use to clean the building in Baxter. I glance at my Bride of Frankenstein's wig and the white dress draped over the corner of my bed and turn on the computer. The end of the day, the night, and October slips away like silk through hands. Three more hours until the new month.

The computer screen lights up, its fan whirring, and the image of Ray and me locked in arms on the mountaintop brightens as much as the light through the trees behind us. We stand on a slate-white rock ground flooded with the sun settling over the landscape sinking into shadows and snow behind us. I wear gloves, my heavy coat, and a scarf as red as a robin's breast. Ray bumped off some frost and set the camera in the bottom of a low, U-shaped tree limb jutting from an old hickory stump. We

OCTOBER

could have stood on the opposite side of the cliff, near the road where the shuttle dropped us off, but had we done that, the sun would have blinded us, and if we had moved too far to the side, where the trails and the forest began, we would have captured the cabin, but the day's late shadows would have obscured us and the wide view. Our suitcase waits by our cabin's front door.

When we stepped out of the van that shuttled us up from Tubersville, the mountain light lengthened Ray, straightening the slouch in his spine before his relapse. He was so lost in light he nearly forgot to tip the driver. But he was my Ray. Strength in his arms returned. He walked on his own, and I certainly did not hold him. His legs stabilized, he was awake in many different ways, and his dark eyes brightened as he stared into the horizon.

He angled the camera until he fit his body in the frame, started the timer, and as fast as his pains allowed, scuttled back to my side before it went off. He draped his arm over me. No plastic band encircled his wrist—nothing about his name, his date of birth, medication warnings, or his being a hospital patient in the cancer ward. Before I wrapped my arms around his ribs, I glanced at the leaves on the ground and wondered if they could predict anything about our future, were I to read them and not hear what the doctors had been telling us about Ray's prognosis. I ran my hands beneath his rib cage and across his bloated stomach. His body was ours, not merely his because it was his or mine, because I was his wife, but ours because of the past bringing us to that point. He winced when I latched onto him. He looked down at me, smiled, and calmed his breath. The camera held us, the tree held the camera, and the day held the tree. The timer's blinking quickened. We kissed and stared into the flash. Like Saul's photo, everything in the photo of Ray and me at our get-away is illuminated.

Before the picture, Ray wore his stocking cap, but he took it off after we walked from the shuttle, wheezing from the effort. Once he saw the view and our home in Cole far down and many miles away, he relished it as vapors rose from the heat of his head chemotherapy had turned bald. The surrounding mountaintop trees remained leafless but swelled with buds waiting for spring. We had arrived at this overlook, and taking that photo, after ooh-ing and ah-ing at the elevation and the scenery, was our first thing. We said it was our second honeymoon. Twenty-seven years had passed since our first one. We had talked about a second that would reaffirm our vows, but we were busy with work and chores filling our calendar until medical appointments took over.

We considered other places we had talked so much about over the years. Exploring waves, sand, and beach life mesmerized us. Both of us grew up landlocked. Ray had seen part of the Gulf, where some of his family lived outside Mobile, but he said, scampering his fingers like crabs, Gulf life is not the same as ocean life.

OCTOBER

"Wanna stop?" he asked while we sat in traffic after an oncologist appointment. He threw his chin at the parking garage for one of Taylor's big shopping malls.

"Are you hungry? Tired?"

"I figured while we're here we could see what they have. Maybe it will decide for us."

We hit every department store that mall had. He tried on several pairs of swimming trunks—some wild floral-prints a Californian would showcase; some plain and suited for an old man looking to meet ladies at the senior-living home's pool before Bingo.

The dressing-room door flew open, and there he stood with his shirt off and wearing flip-flops. He was ready to leave that very minute for the beach. His stomach's scar remained pink and thick, and loose skin dangled over the waistband. Overall his skin wasn't as dark as it had been, save for the bags under his eyes. Extending his pinkie and thumb like a surfer, he said, "Catch a wave, dude!" His voice sounded like it had been to a far-away coast while flying inside an airline cabin full of smoke and sick people coughing on each other.

Lying in bed, we fantasized about the ocean, especially about its magic at night. Darkness turned the beach black, and the waves, illuminated by the moon, cast themselves like mist sparkling sand and rocks while the beach slipped away with each wave but returned when another wave brought it back. Ray wanted to float in the middle of water and inside all that energy.

"Do you want the ocean to take you somewhere?" I asked, my head on his chest.

"It can't." He stroked my hair. "It can't take me anywhere, but it can make me feel like I'm floating when it takes so much to move me."

The body Ray would have brought to the water was the same he wanted to leave on land, but the water could not wash away time, and our talks believed in the power of an ocean sunset. Where else would our bodies have mattered more but when they entered water? He cried when we talked about this. And when he didn't want me to see him cry, he quickly mentioned driving a car along a scenic highway overlooking the ocean on our way to a beachfront hotel, going on and on about the cliffs tumbling into the sea and the peace of crashing waves.

But Ray's health requiring most of our money nixed a trip to the ocean, which would have been our furthest and most expensive.

"Maybe we should go there." He coughed as he chuckled and threw his eyes at the graphic of the Zia sun glowing on the computer screen. "A medicine man in the desert could give me some peyote and knock this cancer out once and for all."

OCTOBER

"There's an entire site devoted to homeopathic treatment in the greater Albuquerque area. Santa Fe has *a lot* more options. Cactus juice and melted snow in a commemorative cup."

"Shoot, that's all I need." His braced himself on my chair. "I bet that cup costs more than the stuff they dump in it. Silver?"

"'Metals selected for their healing properties from sacred locations as determined by pre-Columbian history, indigenous tribal oral traditions, and circle-energy rites,'" I read from the website. "One-of-a-kind, it says."

"If that's true, then I would love to buy up some swampland for sale in that desert out there." Before he started for the bedroom, he said, "The accounts department at the hospital would sure miss our business."

"The nurses in radiology would miss you. That's for sure."

"I still got it."

"You still do."

He winked at me, sashayed his hips, and closed the bedroom door.

But traveling from Cole to New Mexico required flying. Ray had flown several times for conferences for Blue Sky, but I had never flown. And after we considered him being trapped in a flying metal tube and needing to stop, we looked elsewhere. We could have knocked out seeing the ocean by driving to the Atlantic and the cities on our side of the country, stopping along the way for both of us to take a break. But reaching the mountains near us required neither driving nor flying.

9

The place off the highway served breakfast all day and devoted a menu to two pages of nothing but breakfast, which was the talk of the town when they opened. Ray was so happy with his two eggs, two biscuits with apple butter, and two slabs of bacon. He drenched his plate in syrup, the flood of which stuck the peppercorns to his eggs. He devoured his meal and gulped down several cups of coffee. He hadn't eaten that way in so long. And then with tickets in hand, we boarded the train that early Sunday morning at Cole's station and headed for the mountains.

The next stop after Cole was Tubersville in the foothills where we grabbed some supplies and boarded a van that shuttled us to the cabin. We joked we should have bought a third ticket for Ray's cancer because, although no one on that train would have seen it, it rode free of charge.

Spring was on its way down in the valley, but winter lingered in the higher elevation where cool temps kept snow and frost on rocks and trees. Local lore said the law would never find criminals if they hid up there in the mountains, and the mountains would eat them up before the law could.

The train's whistle blew as we turned a corner. Cole drifted behind us. Our speed picked up. We ate our snacks I had in my backpack, but Ray mainly stuck with protein drinks because he wanted to keep building his strength after surgery and they were easy on his stomach. We played Go Fish with his stack of Taylor University cards with the Golden Knights mascot striking various poses, pointing his giant puffy gloved finger and flexing his biceps after a touchdown, or wearing glasses with books by his side while typing on a computer.

The landscape changed from flat woodlands and pockets of prairie to slopes of snow-crusted trees and gray tones. Ray glanced over and smiled after I pulled out my romance book I bought at Last Pages Used Books in Cole a few days before we left. I had another book in my bag for this trip, one Gloria loaned to me and said I had to read.

"I'm going to defend them until I am no longer on this earth," I said to him, flipping a page where the heroine resented her big-city life, six-figure salary, and exhausting ambition and wanted to move back to her hometown to run a coffeeshop all while fearing her past would find her.

"And I'm gonna smile my toothy smile at you about those books until I am no longer on this earth."

Trees rushing by and the clacking tracks filled the silence growing between us.

OCTOBER

"You give me all I need, but I need to read about some gal who has her head in the clouds and meets a man who doesn't really exist."

"True. And that gal doesn't really either except in the pages of a made-up world where apparently you get everything you want. All the sugar without none of the calories." He grinned before returning to the landscape.

Cars on the highway matched our speed for a little bit, and then we all broke off for our separate paths. One of those cars could have been us—the one hovering over concrete and behind the train's glass before vanishing when a tunnel pitched in black covered us.

"I can't think of a time, other than seeing in-laws, when we'll be together for several days in a place that's not ours," he said once the train crossed out of the tunnel, out of Cole County, and approached the state line.

I looked at him over the pages of my book. "We could drive each other crazy."

"That's already happened."

"We were in your sister's place when that hurricane blew through, and our flight was canceled."

"Yeah." He closed his eyes. Shadows from the trees thickening in the valley flicked over his face. "We were also at your mom's place when the cows from that field behind her got out and ended up in her yard."

"That's right. Dad had passed by then. He would have laughed so hard at that. 'Lee! We can have fresh milk whenever we want.' He would have gone out there with a bucket of hay cubes and hand fed them."

"Your mom was cool as a cucumber."

"She had Dad's sense of humor late in life. If it had happened before that, she would have been out there slapping those cows on their butts and trying to get them back on their side of the fence."

The train was about an hour from the Tubersville station. We crossed in and out of several counties where they met like corners of a jigsaw puzzle patched together by snow and black ground with green shoots.

"Mom had this little plastic spotted cow magnet on her fridge in her apartment at the senior center. Dad gave it to her for one of her birthdays. She laughed out loud and kissed him while holding that cow."

None of the other passengers noticed me when I laughed at the memory. They had headphones in, watched movies, read, or dozed off with the train's cradle and hum. "She never used it. It never held anything, smack dab in the middle of the fridge. It was always there by itself."

Ray said, "Mom once gave Dad a pair of cooking tongs and told him, 'You either stop complaining about my cooking, or get

OCTOBER

your you-know-what in that kitchen and find out what you come up with. We'll wait.'"

"She was a great cook."

"She was, except when she went off-script, which was too often." Rubbing his eyes, he leaned his chair back and slipped on his sweater. "Dad was used to good ol' fashioned home-cooking. Fried, sugared, and salted, but she wanted to try all these new things. Fondue, Italian, French desserts, Brazilian meats, which sent his sodium levels through the roof. Us kids were just happy to eat, except for that Chinese-Southern fusion she once tried. Sweet-and-sour sauce on collard greens made us all visit the bathroom that night. She said, 'What was it? Too much soy? Ginger? Can't be the ginger. Y'all like ginger,'" Ray said in a loud high-pitched, quick-tempo voice, laughing so hard he cleared his throat. "My dad yelled from the pot, 'Sharon, baby, it's too much! Take us back to what we know and love!' I went to school the next day and had to excuse myself about every fifteen minutes. The teacher kept giving me a sink eye about it. But I wasn't about to tell her what was going on. She wouldn't have believed me anyway. '"You're trying to get out of class, Mr. Pemberton.' Carla said her love life was ruined because her boyfriend at the time didn't want to be around her."

"I bet she kept that grudge against your mom."

"Oh, good Lord, you have no idea. Plus, she was a blossoming young woman. It was like walking through a mine field with heavy boots that could set off something as meek as a deer. You could misstep anywhere, anytime…and believe me, we all did. Add into the mix she was trying to watch her figure."

"But she made it through."

"She made it through. She dated What's His Name for a while and moved on. D'wayne, I think, was his name. 'Dee-wayne No Mane,' R.J. said because he was going bald so young." Ray laughed so hard he wiped his eyes. "He was no good for her anyway. She's done better since. Way better. Miss Lawyer up there in Atlanta now."

The train climbed some more and leveled out where the valley curved, and then the mountains came into view. The car's windows frosted before we pulled into Tubersville. Its charm, restaurants, and shops tempted us to stay, but our van waited to shuttle us to the top of the mountain and our cabin.

• • •

The driver helped Ray with the suitcases before saying goodbye and pocketing his tip. On his way down the driveway, he stopped the van, backed up it up, and said, "Next Sunday, right?" Ray nodded and waved him on. Two honks from the van. And then we posed for our photo.

The cabin was fully furnished with one large master bedroom, built-in bookcases, entertainment, and property secluded enough to keep the outside world away, including, I

OCTOBER

hoped, any bears coming out of hibernation. At one time, the cabin's owner must have thought mountain living and styles from the 1970s made a strong combination. Part of me enjoyed the outdated clash. When we first met, Ray had prominent sideburns and often wore his shirts unbuttoned a few buttons down from his butterfly collar where his chest hair curled over the polyester fabric of a shirt so faintly blue a bird fancier would have mistaken it for the surface of a large egg laid by a giant robin.

Ray wheeled our suitcases into the master bedroom where the daylight had yet to reach, but outside the windows, the mountains and trees were visible inside blues and grays.

Opening the kitchen curtains stirred up dust. The tomatoes and green peppers printed on them tinted the mounds of snow packed against the wall stretching into the backyard.

"Do you smell natural gas?"

Ray sniffed the air near the stove. "No, but I'll take a look."

The remaining curtains were orange-brown plaids at the front of the living room and large crimson ones covering the long windows at the back.

Ray hugged me from behind. "Some big pines back there. Cut those down and make something out of them. Take it back with us."

"Like what?"

"I don't know. Something."

"The property owners may not like that."

"I can see another cabin way down there at the end of those shadows."

"Maybe we're not alone."

"We might run into them." Coughing, he stared deeper into the landscape.

"They got trails around here. They touch a state park that's got caves, streams, and lots of trees you can't chop down and take back with you." I leaned into his chest. "There's a lake out there."

He kissed me and walked to the living room shelves filled with CDs, cassettes, LPs, VHS tapes, and DVDs. "Quite a selection. Including this one." His fingers stopped walking the options. He set a record on the turntable and closed the lid.

"Always and forever your number-one pick," I said as the song's first notes from a trumpet floated to us and up, gliding over the middle of the living room.

"Can't never go wrong with Miles." He kissed me again. "You, that view, this record…this'll be a great week."

Kind of Blue drifted from the two speakers by the desk and the two mounted over the TV in the corners of the living room. Those notes from that LP were standard in our place in Cole, and in the cabin, their back-and-forth motion lifted me like I was a fragment returned to its larger stone.

The afternoon Sunday light poured in through the curtains, and when it did, something else entered the cabin. I wasn't sure

OCTOBER

what it was, but it was something like the past, the present, and the future all wrapped in one and carried to where we stood and where that presence waited to emerge and expand when the time was right. If I hadn't welcomed it when it poured through the windows or if I hadn't pulled back the curtains, it still would have emptied itself through the glass and the fabric, warmed my skin, and settled inside those walls around and the floor underneath us. We weren't supposed to be anywhere else.

* * *

A crackling fireplace and its smells woke me. The bedroom clock said after eleven in the morning. I stepped first into the living room and then into the kitchen eat-in. Ray had resealed the bathroom faucet, adjusted the toilet, replaced lightbulbs, tightened some of the loose cupboard doors, and re-secured the line to the stove. The smell of natural gas had disappeared. He grinned at me.

"You've been busy."

"Want some lunch? Late breakfast?"

"Where did you find that?" I nodded at a toolbox.

"The shed."

I followed his eyes toward the backyard but couldn't see clearly because he hadn't fully opened one of the curtains. "Excuse me," I said after a giant yawn. "I guess I needed my rest. I didn't hear you at all."

"That means I can slip in and out of here without you noticing. Maybe I walked down to the lake, cut down a pine, and turned it into this fire."

"Oh, did you?"

"Maybe I went to town and came back."

"How? The train? The van come get you?"

"Maybe something else."

"What?"

He shrugged his shoulders. "Maybe I got dinner." His finger tapped the window behind the desk near the curtain panel blocking my view. "Big ol' buck walked by the shed, I stepped out, all that firewood in my arms, and he and I had a talk, but it didn't last too long. I said, 'Why don't you stay for dinner?' And he said, 'OK.'"

"Where is he?" My glasses slid to the end of my nose.

"Out there," he replied, trying not to laugh.

"The shed?"

"Mmm. He's waiting."

"For you to put him out of his misery?"

"Humanely."

I pulled back the curtains. "I don't know about a buck in there."

"He's in there. I went out there and saw him for myself after I got the firewood. There's more in there." His voice was clear and soft. He stood up and moved the toolbox by the back door

OCTOBER

before washing his hands when the microwave dinged. He handed me a mug of coffee. "I'm gonna grab a quick bite to eat and write to R.J. and Tasha, if I still have it in me when I get there."

"You should."

"And I'm thinking tomorrow I'll write to Carla and John. Maybe Uncle Zippy. I need to. It's been too long."

"They'll all be so happy to hear from you."

"I'll mail them when we get back to Cole. But if I don't get around to writing them today, I can save them for later this week. Won't be my last letters."

We smiled at each other after I took a long sip. The silence between us on the train followed us here.

He grabbed a plate for his sandwich before rummaging for a pen and notepad in the desk drawers. He rubbed his eyes and stared at the blank pages. For several minutes, he scribbled, scratched out whatever he scribbled, scribbled again, sighed, and tossed the notepad on the desk.

"Don't break yourself," I said sitting at the eat-in table with a bowl of cereal and the novel Gloria loaned me. "They don't have to be all at once."

He walked into the kitchen for a cup of hot cocoa. "Marshmallows would be good in this."

"I don't think there's any here." I opened some cupboards. "Animals might find them when the place isn't used."

"Imagine coming home to that."

"You can put them in the shed out there with your buck. We can have our own zoo."

After scanning the backyard, he chuckled and, with his pen and paper, flopped back to the couch. "But only after we have deer steaks tonight."

I unpacked a few of the bags we hadn't emptied yesterday. "I don't think we picked up any at the store."

"Deer steaks?"

"Marshmallows."

"It's all right. Next time we're here."

I smiled at his response and tightened my robe. He sat with his back to me. Amber light brightened the side of his head closest to the window where he peered at the shed. After several minutes of no writing, he jotted down a few things until he fell asleep in the couch. I stood over his shoulder. His letter made it as far as the date and a few lines of writing to say hi and things were on the up and up for us in our home-away-from-home for the week in the mountains. *On a break from chemo and recovery. Patty needs this as much as I do. Docs are cautiously optimistic without sugarcoating anything about what's ahead.* He snored. He always snored, but since his surgery and treatment, pain forced him to be on his back, which brought on apnea, but he also couldn't sleep long because of his stomach healing. If cancer wasn't the cause of his death, we had joked his snoring and lack of sleep—

OCTOBER

and then my lack of sleep because of him—would do him in. His pen fell to the floor, rolled to the desk's feet, and wedged itself between a gash in the wood and a string of light after it moved to that side of the cabin, in from the curtains.

Watching him sleep, I wondered if he knew night was approaching and that, yes, with the doctor's odds, one more night up here and with me would not be his last, nor would tomorrow, nor would the next day until the week was up and we packed up and returned to Cole. Did he know several afternoons would approach him and me and they wouldn't lead toward the last night but would remind us about cherishing any light—sun or moon—before another hour, day, or season chased it away? He was not a patient, at least not someone stuck in a hospital bed, under the knife, or chained to monitoring devices, nor did he want to be called a survivor or a warrior, as some of the emails and mail he received put it. I don't know how these organizations found him, but they sure would love to have our financial support by buying a memento, which he could wear, molded in plastic and, for a discounted fee, branded with important dates, such as when he fought and won his battle against cancer, or a message, such as a Bible verse or powerful saying, getting him through the toughest moments.

Before closing the curtains to shield Ray, I stared past where he slept. Snow on a tree branch outside the cabin's living room window glimmered like a bright stone. Paint flecked off in places on the metal shed where weather and time had eaten away. For a moment, in the remaining morning light, the shed's two front doors and its sides bulged from every invisible thing packed inside. Squat to the ground, its cold colors and silhouette made it tomb-like, tall and wide enough for many things to move around in after finding rest there. Light sliced through some of the rusted-out holes in the shed. Boxes of memories could fit in there. A buck could too. A doe and her fawn could fit in there. As could a person.

 I stretched out in the recliner next to the couch with the book. "She's real good," Gloria said, handing its tattered cover to me. "I'm a big fan. And Bobbie Ann's an appropriate name for a Kentucky gal." On the train ride to the cabin, my heart sank a little when I read the synopsis. The protagonist was a breast-cancer survivor. Gloria left a message on my phone, which I couldn't listen to because we lost signals, but once we stopped at Tubersville for the shuttle, I listened to it at the station. "Oh, girl, I am so sorry. I wasn't thinking." Her message paused. "But you know what, it was my heart, not my head, doing the talking. It's meant to be, Patty. Trust me on this. That book is meant to be. And if you find out I'm wrong, then I will say I am sorry the next time we talk, and you can watch me eat a whole pie of crow. Love you and Ray. Bill says hi and sends his love too. Have a great time. See you soon."

OCTOBER

Like the woman in the novel, Ray lived with his cancer, didn't shy away from it, or expected to be treated any differently because of it. Life moved on without drama as it had when the cancer wasn't front and center. The woman accepted an end was coming, and she had neither a specific time nor a place for the coming end. Ray and I had visited a lawyer and the bank. He talked with his supervisor and the HR department at Blue Sky. And yet through all those moments leading up to and after his surgery, up to him asleep in the couch with his half-started letter, he never knew what to say to his family.

Light warmed the curtains, intensifying their crimson. Ray's head slumped deeper into sleep. His body quivered, and I may not have been with him in that dream, where he may have had a full head of hair, a beard, and a life similar to but different from the one he left behind as he dreamt—not sweating from using the bathroom without my help, moving from hospital room to tests, or eating his favorite foods without throwing up later. If we were together in his dream, we may have walked near water or land. Maybe we went into the shed. Maybe the sun was out in his dream, as it was inside the cabin, reaching the height of the day and spreading its fingers through the shed. Or maybe his dream was at night where the shed loomed like the mouth to a cave, where light was the same spot for someone to enter and leave by.

* * *

Ray poured two glasses of wine and, after setting them on the eat-in table, raised his to mine. "To us. To you for finding this place. To a not-so-regular evening."

"No Chemo Wednesday."

"No Chemo Wednesday. Looks real yummy, baby." He inhaled so strongly he coughed a bit.

"Thank you. Not too bad with our supplies and what's up here."

"Not at all."

He blessed the food and ate silently for several minutes. He wiped his mouth with his napkin and cleared his throat.

"Listen, I was thinking…we could stay longer, come back some more, and down the line, own the cabin. Maybe move here permanently. There's lots of potential here. I'd be busy, and it'd be good. Knock out a wall over there, new sink, upgrade the appliances, put up some drywall in the master bedroom, heated towel racks in the bathroom, install a jacuzzi outside for the winter days up here. We can keep the couch but update its upholstery. I could re-stain the wood inlays on the arms." His hand trembled when it moved through the air and he described his renovations.

I rotated the wine glass's stem between my fingers. "That's a lot for a vacation home."

"It'd be more than a vacation. It'd be ours."

"We haven't upgraded anything at home in years."

OCTOBER

He chewed rapidly and leaned over the chair, pointing with his fork. "There's that big rock in the back yard. It would fit right here in the middle of the living room."

"A rock?"

"I saw it when you opened the curtains that first day." He threw his eyes over there. "I'd polish it up. Probably three to six months to do something like that. This place could be like a Frank Lloyd Wright." His swallowed so hard he grabbed water. "What would it take to make this place feel like home and not a get-away?"

"Where will we get the supplies to do all this?"

"Cole Hardware."

"Cole Hardware!" I laughed out loud, nearly choking on my wine. "That'll be a *l-o-n-g* string of projects. We'll either keep them financially stable for years to come, or we'll belly them up."

"Or Lowe's or Home Depot in Taylor."

"And the money?"

He dumped the remaining potatoes from the glass dish onto his plate and added a sprig of rosemary that missed my chopping, breaking it apart with hands calloused from his projects and time going to and from the shed. He pushed around bones from the chicken. "We can cash in our IRAs."

"We're not doing that."

"We're not exactly adding to them right now after what happened."

"We took out a second mortgage for your surgery."

"Patty, please don't get me wrong. Why not put it to better use?"

"Our future isn't 'better use' when we're old and in need of who knows what."

He opened his arms to the cabin and looked around the space. "This can be our future."

"Ray."

"We can figure it out. Sooner rather than later. We'll make trips here and back. We sell the house in Cole."

"What if we came up here every now and then, like we did with this. We could make it every three months or so. Maybe once a month. That sounds OK with me."

"If we did that, we could bring stuff up here, make it more permanent. Maybe we could get a longer lease like a timeshare. I can talk to the owner."

"How will we get stuff up here?"

"The train. Or we could drive it. If we're staying here, we can make lots of trips."

"Are we staying or having a vacation home?"

"Staying would be pretty good," he said before coughing into his fist. His cough intensified until veins pulsed in his throat and darkened his face. He braced himself on the table. His eyes turned bloodshot. He sat back down.

OCTOBER

I started heating water on the stove for lemon-herb tea for him.

"We'll take turns," he whispered.

"Doing what?"

"You driving, me driving. That train won't let us bring much but our suitcases. I don't think we can get your grandma's hutch on board or my great aunt's clock either." He cleared his throat again. "We can throw all our furniture in the back of our car. Tools in my lap for that rock and the stuff in the shed."

I glanced at him.

"There are things in there I want to tackle. It hasn't been touched in years." Ray turned his body until he faced the living room. It was night, but the curtains were open, and he stared into the darkness. "We'll find a way up here." He coughed some more.

"Let's talk about something else." Patting his forehead, I said, "You feel warm."

"It's the fireplace."

"No, I think you have a fever."

"There's no thermometer in the bathroom." His voice raised. "We should've picked up one in Tubersville."

"We don't need one. Take it easy. We're here to relax."

The kettle piped, and I poured him his drink.

"Getting an ambulance up here would be a sight to see. But what a view once they got up here!"

"I don't find that funny."

He looked at me, and his lips parted for a few seconds before drinking. "OK. Bad joke. Dessert and our movie?"

"Yes, please." I kissed his cheek, gathering the dishes.

From the freezer he pulled out the package of Thin Mints he bought from the Girl Scouts while we waited for the shuttle at Tubersville. He ate a few, dumped the rest in a bowl he had set on the end-table by the couch, and with hands on hips, cruised the DVDs. Marx Brothers, Laurel and Hardy, some of the *Die Hard* series—"How many did they make?" he laughed—travel videos about the castles of England, Ireland, Scotland, and Wales. One of the sports documentaries was about the Chicago Bulls' dynasty of the 1990s. Ray followed them for the entire decade, knew all the players and their stats, and while watching the games, acted as an unpaid teammate or a volunteer assistant coach offering his ball-handling skills or tactics from his vantage point on the couch. "They never listen to me," he said whether the Bulls won or lost.

"How's this?"

As hot water and bubbles filled the kitchen sink, I looked at the cover. A runner crossed the finish line as joy rose from pain on his face and in his body. *Simultaneously heartbreaking and jubilant. A profile of courage, forgiveness, sacrifice. A triumph of the human spirit.* I stopped reading when the synopsis mentioned the runner refused to run on Sundays because it was the Lord's day. He chose

OCTOBER

missionary work over running. His life ended in a Japanese internment camp during World War II.

"Do you want something else?" Ray walked back to the living room and opened the cabinets. "A game?" He motioned to another shelf. "Monopoly? Chutes and Ladders?"

"If that's what you want. The movie's fine."

"What do you want to do?"

"Relax with you in our cabin. We said at dinner this is not our normal Wednesday. I don't want you worked up over this."

After crunching a cookie, he slurped some tea, powered on the TV and DVD player, and walking back to the kitchen, grabbed a towel. One dish slipped between us and shattered on the floor, chipping the tile and exposing the old darkened paste between each square.

"I'll be back," he said, setting on the counter the chip like an island picked up by invisible hands.

"You can save it for tomorrow."

The back door opened and closed. A light glowed inside the shed before clicking off. The back door opened and closed again. A bottle of glue thumped on the floor where the faded black lines ran their dark canals beneath us. He covered the patch with a piece of paper and blue tape he went back into the shed for.

"Just watch you step until it's dry. Probably tomorrow. I'll check before we go to bed."

I nodded and smiled.

He returned the tape and glue to the shed. Several minutes passed before the light in there turned off and he returned.

We sat on the couch. Ray pushed play on the remote. The documentary about the missionary who refused to run on Sundays started.

The moon shone behind the curtains. If we owned this cabin or rented it every month and threw parties, how many people would fit? Would they drive up here? Would they boost ticket sales for the trains? Nanette Wilson would love Tubersville's old main street and would never make it past the many antique shops.

The image of the runner paused on the screen—his arms out and down by his side, like an inverted V, his fists clenched, and yet his entire body appeared loose and determined to reach an ultimate destination. His chin was high, his eyes closed, as though he ran not along a track with his colleagues, the press, and the crowds surrounding him but ran alone into ecstasy.

I slid closer to Ray, and he tightened the quilt over us. Several pieces of popcorn missed my mouth and lay between a paisley-yellow pinwheel and a rose-tinted one stitched across the top.

How many people would come here if he died here? Would this cabin be the site for a memorial? If we didn't own it, could we rent it for something like that—and in time for the service? But what if he were he to die here? Would I be able to enter the cabin? Would it remain as something we did together but I could never return to, the curtains long drawn shut?

OCTOBER

. . .

Thursday morning, I couldn't find Ray. A dream of us riding in a car didn't help, and when the dream shook me out of sleep, he wasn't in bed or the bedroom. I rushed toward the door as though a long hall stretched between me and the rest of the cabin, as though the cabin was multi-layered, spread out, and big enough to hide him. "Jesu, Joy of Man's Desiring" played on the living-room speakers, but Ray wasn't there. Beams of morning light cut through smoke filling the kitchen. The coffee pot bubbled. Sausage crackled in a pan. Eggs rested on a cutting board. The table had napkins, silverware, and jars of jelly and butter. Under a paper towel, a knife dipped in the jelly lay on the counter.

I opened the back door and yelled at a shadow passing outside the window and going into the shed. "Ray?"

"Morning, honey." He spun around, the shed's floor creaking, and crunched something in his mouth while moving a rusted camping lantern, climbing rope, and snowshoes until they sat on a cardboard box near him. He used no gloves and, underneath his robe, had had on the sweatpants and t-shirt he wore to bed.

"You want your coat?" I asked him, shivering as I made my way to the front of the shed. With its chipped green paint and rusted hinges, it was spacious enough to stand and move around, dodging boxes and bins. Lawn and garden supplies. Tools, extension cords, motor oil, a riding lawn mower in the corner.

Wooden and hand-made shelves stood in another corner—crooked, leaning one way, shellac-smooth in some patches, rotting and rough in others.

"I was stepping out here for a sec." His breath curled in the air. Finishing the last bite of toast topped with red jelly, he licked his fingers. "Breakfast is almost ready." He rearranged some more items. The ground's moisture had darkened the bottom of his sweatpants and soles of his slippers.

The oven timer beeped. I glanced over my shoulder while Ray inspected a blue-and-orange metal hiking stick topped with a polished silver knob, bright inside the darkened shed. It looked barely used. Ray twirled it in his hands, pushing out his lips and staring at it as he did. I tightened my robe and started for the kitchen.

"It's the second loaf," Ray said, setting down the stick and kissing me on my cheek. "How'd you sleep?"

"What time did you get up?"

"I was out, but then I had to get up. I came out here." He moved bags of mulch from one spot in the shed to another, stacking them. "I fixed some toast to hold me over until you were up."

"I don't remember you doing that."

Ray moved a red climbing rope from behind Christmas ornaments and organized some tools on wall pegs. "Coffee?"

OCTOBER

"Yes, please. Thank you." I stared at wood-carving supplies and sandpaper he pulled out. "Let me clean up before we eat."

He scraped his slippers on the door mat, frost and snow flaking off, and took out the bread from the oven. Cinnamon swirled in the air. He sliced it and slid hunks of butter in between each four slices for us. He rinsed jelly from the knife and threw away the paper towel.

The mirror by the back door reflected me as I walked toward the bathroom. Because of my dream's intensity, my face looked like it had been puffed up and then drained until the skin around my eyes and jaw hung down like wet dough. The bed's mattress hadn't helped much either. It had done a number on my back, hips, and hamstrings. Even after four nights of finding my nest in that mattress, and having Ray next to me, rather than him sleeping in the hospital or in the other bedroom in our house in Cole, no position made me comfortable.

In my dream, Ray and I rode in a car cruising along the edge of a seawall, the slope of which loomed behind us. The car never veered off the edge, nor did its lack of space frighten me. We sat in the back. The driver was anonymous, a silhouette. The full moon hovered over the water, and that single source of light illuminated the topmost layer of the ocean like a thin silver line running east-west until the blackened waves overtook it at the furthest points on the horizon, where the water lost any silver reflection, and reached the rocks in ink-like washes. Ray and I were the only things in color. Everything else was toned in grays, blacks, and whites, as though a film from long ago bled from its frames.

Hands resting in his lap, Ray turned to me. He sat behind the driver's seat. "You can't always turn around where you are," he said, pointing his forefinger behind my right shoulder and lowering his head just enough as though something or someone stood by my side.

I stared at him and his finger but did not look anywhere else. Pieces of moonlight crossed his face and shifted it from a middle-aged Ray to an older Ray. As I turned to my right, Ray faced forward. The black water rushed by the car. I pivoted in the back seat, and before the driver came into view, that portion of the car was missing, like a giant mouth had bit it off, which exposed the night and the road flying underneath us. Wind whipped my hair, pulling it into the night and up toward a field of lights twinkling in the distance where the land crumbled into the ocean and where the stars could be seen without anything blocking them below, in the middle, or above.

Before I reached the cabin's bathroom, I grabbed a kitchen towel and stopped to wipe up drops of water from Ray's shoes and the bottom of his sweatpants that made a trail between the back door and the kitchen floor. My heart nearly stopped. I bent down at dark spots pooling on the floor—strawberry jelly, not blood.

OCTOBER

Ray devoured his eggs and bacon and slurped down his coffee. He bobbed his head back and forth to the music on the living-room speakers matching his eating's steady pace. The food in front of me was a meal I enjoyed making on a regular basis when Ray got ready for work—eggs, meat, and toast—and when the smells of breakfast and his cologne mixed. Sitting next to him as husband and wife, as lovers, as friends was part of a new day's promise. I did not hear from him until lunchtime when I microwaved my food in the library's employee lounge and talked to him on the phone. I called him at the hospice before or after I ate because we planned our lunches at the same time. But the cabin in the mountains was not our house, and neither the cabin nor the mountains were near Cole. The appliances were modern, sleek, and uniform in their stainless-steel lineup. The arrangement of the windows, cabinets, and table were different, and yet Ray reading the newspaper and sitting there with him carried to me what we had elsewhere.

Rubbing my arm, he said, "We should get out today. Go to the lake. Lunch, some coffee, maybe a small bottle of bourbon." His eyes darted to the side of the liquor cabinet.

"If you feel like it, sure."

"I do."

"I'll make some sandwiches."

"I'll do it." He shot up, pivoting on the foot and leg that troubled him after surgery. With one hop, he propelled from the table and toward the fridge. "I bet we can get there by noon."

"Are you in a race?"

"We've been cooped up in here. It's supposed to be beautiful today." He grabbed the cabin key and tied it to a piece of the red climbing rope he cut in the shed. He looped the rope, slid his wrist through, and cinched it tightly against his skin before sliding on his sweater and laying his coat and stocking cap on the back of the couch. He set our shoes by the front door. "I was always talking about this when I was bed-ridden. Like the old days at the Chickataw."

Once out the front door and down the driveway, we turned right at the end of the hill where the van had shuttled us up.

"Hold on." Ray walked to the back of the cabin, where the shed door opened and, after several seconds, closed. Carrying the metal hiking stick, he returned to where I waited. "We're no spring chickens."

"But I am younger than you," I said, holding his hand when he offered it.

"You're forever thirty, whereas I reach sixty-five a little more every day."

"It'll be a milestone."

"With you, anything and everything is." He smiled at me in the quiet patch of trees and gravel peeling off toward the woods.

OCTOBER

Trails signs told us our options. An easy two-mile loop was the first one and wound around the cabins on the property and touched the edges of the state park. The second sign said PERFECT FOR A SHORT DAY HIKE – NOT TOO STRENUOUS – OUT-AND-BACK. The lake trail was the longest, and its sign reminded us during the warm months to watch out for ticks and mosquitos and during the winter months to be aware of icy patches especially near and around Lake Merritt. In big red letters, the last line on the sign said During All Months Except Winter Beware Bears.

"I'll make myself as big as I can if we come across Momma Bear." Ray shook his arms overhead, but he couldn't lift them as high as he used to. He puffed himself out as much as he could, but he was too skinny to appear menacing. He looked like a trail runner who didn't want to break his pace while a larger, predatory mammal let him know who really owned the woods. He winced and rubbed his shoulder. "I guess I need to warm up first."

"If we see Momma Bear, she will have her way with us. Did the shed have any bear spray?" I looked up the road from where we came. Far behind us, the cabin stood out like a little brown box against a wintry background. We could have turned around without losing too much time. The day was still early and, to our benefit, getting longer.

"I didn't see anything. There were some boxes of bullets but no rifle."

"We don't need you bringing a gun."

"Oh, come on now." He glared at me and lowered his chin until his whiskers whitened in the light. He blew on his hands, which had stopped trembling after he lowered his arms. "We'd go out as legends. The news'll say we died fighting a bear."

I made a face.

"I'm just pokin' your side. They're probably all still asleep. I bet every one of them is snoring. Dad because he's too fat from eating while the leaves turned color. Lots of carbs to gain weight to keep him warm. Mom because she wants to rest from taking care of everybody. And the kids are like teenagers. Too lazy to do anything until their parents force them, which means they sleep until noon. Mom probably nudges their bear butts along while Dad lounges under a tree with a honey-bee hive stuck to his paws, and he's wishing he could go back to sleep after seeing all that in front of him."

I laughed with him.

"Besides, it's March."

"But still winter. Not spring yet."

"OK, they're starting to stir. They know spring is on its way, like us. We'll stay vigilant." He adjusted his glasses and fidgeted with his stocking cap.

"Keep it off. You don't want to wear it anyway."

He stuffed it in his coat's pocket. "I promise I won't get sick."

"You can't promise that."

OCTOBER

We looked down the trial leading to the lake. The air pricked our skin. A lot of miles to and from, but the path looked like it was out of a fairy tale, especially one with a happy ending—dreamy with bright backlight and trees as the sun continued rising and taking away the cold and darkness inhabiting the woods. The morning was warmer than when we ate breakfast. Birdsongs were more frequent, and a few robins flitted in and out of branches and shrubs. Hope filled the buds of every tree surviving winter.

"Good morning," a man's deep and raspy voice boomed behind us.

We spun in place. A couple came up the trail.

"Good morning," we replied.

"Lovely morning for a walk."

"It sure is."

"We're getting in our two miles for the day and one more before dinner." He stuck out his hand. "Bill."

"Ray. We just started."

The two men nodded and shook hands. Bill may have been the same age as Ray or older. He was stockier and wider in the shoulders like a bowling ball set on top of legs narrowing from the hips down and settling into feet much larger than his hands. His thick mustache was all white, he wore a red jacket with white trim, and if he had grown a beard, with the chestnut-shaped red nose jutting out from his face, he would have been Santa Claus.

"My wife, Sheila."

"Hello there." Her face wrinkled when she smiled. Two braids of ash-blonde hair curled beneath a sunhat with a vibrant ribbon tied around its base. Shiny gold and silver pins spread across the upturned brim. GREAT SMOKEY MOUNTAINS, APPALACHIAN TRAIL, THE EVERGLADES, RED RIVER SANCTUARY, MARK TWAIN NATIONAL FOREST, SHENANDOAH NATIONAL PARK.

"Patty. Very nice to meet you."

"I believe you all showed up around the same day we did," Bill said. "We saw you at the shuttle stop a few days ago before when got on ours."

"We were on the next shuttle," Sheila added, rotating her face from Ray to me, her smile squeezing her eyes into a squint. She had a slow drawl like a horse and buggy taking its time and with high tones like steady bells on the harness. "Do you like your cabin?"

"We do," I said. "Very cozy. We're thankful for everything it has."

"We've been coming here for a few years," Bill said. "Heard about it from a coworker of mine. We loved it so much we bought the place when one became available."

Ray's nod agreed.

"We should have been here last weekend. I heard the whole sky was filled with these streaks of light running up and down. Pinks and blues." Bill wagged his finger from sky to horizon. "It

OCTOBER

sounded like quite a sight. Got to be here at the right minute to see those things. They come and go. Some kind of weather effect because spring is right around the corner. Something about the ground temp and reflection."

Ray and I glanced at the skyline above the trees—a never-ending blue sky and a brightening day.

"You said you bought your place?" Ray asked.

"We sure did." Sheila's eyes glistened. "We used to drive up here, but we *love* taking the train."

"Us too. That's the way to do it," I said.

Sheila and Bill hummed a yes.

"Where y'all headed?" she asked.

"The lake."

"Oh, that's a real good walk. Old farts like us need to get the blood pumping, but that's a little dicey for me nowadays. I had heart surgery about six months ago." Bill patted his chest. "Too much good food." He kissed Sheila on the cheek. "But I need to watch it. Some big inclines and declines on the way there. I could probably do it today, feeling good and all. It's not too cold or too warm. But once you get to the bottom of the last decline, the land flattens out into the lake surrounded by all these trees. I don't know how it ended up that way, but it did."

"It's a magical place. We should go down there together."

"That's so sweet of you," I replied to Sheila, "but we haven't done anything like this in a long time. Just the two of us. I need him all to myself." I looped my arm through Ray's arm.

"Oh." She blushed and winked.

"It was nice meeting you." Ray stuck out his hand.

"Yes, sir. And you as well." Bill tapped Ray's hand while shaking it. "Hope to see you up here again."

"That would be great." Ray smiled, glancing at me.

Sheila waved. "We can all get together and have some nice meals and drinks."

I cuddled closer to Ray. "When the time is right for us to come back here, yes, we should."

"We'll be easy to find," Sheila said. "Just down from your place."

"Out our front door, and all we have to do is knock," I said, laughing.

"Or maybe out here again."

"You never know."

"Enjoy that spot." Bill's finger pointed down the trail. "I hope it's all to yourselves."

. . .

After some time passed on the trail, Ray checked his watch. "Twelve-thirty-seven."

"The sign back there said about a quarter mile left."

OCTOBER

"Want some water?" He slung the backpack around and took out the canteen. He pulled one of the small bottles of bourbon from the kitchen's liquor cabinet. "A little extra?"

"Why not?"

Ray groaned using the metal hiking stick to sit on a rock. Sweat dampened his forehead, and he mopped it up with a red bandana he pulled from his back pocket and tied around his neck. Every tendon and joint in his knees cracked and popped when he reached the rock. His breathing leveled but remained heavy like a boat churning in place. I placed one foot on a log to stretch my hamstrings and switched legs. Ray slumped over, his long arms on his knees pulled up to his chest. I picked up the backpack, but Ray latched onto it, coughing as he did.

"I got it," his voice rasped, trying to sound calm and tough at the same time. He kept his eyes on the trail. "One more swig?" He flashed the bourbon.

"No, honey, I'm all thawed out. And I think we're all good." I looked at his sweaty face. "Do you want a little food in your stomach?"

"I'll wait for the lake. We're almost there." He kicked some of the dry leaves until wet ones turned up. "You know about punk?"

"I haven't heard that since Dad and his brothers. 'A dog's ear keeps punk wood dry.'"

"That's right." He pointed to old wet wood underneath some of the leaves, scraped it off, and showed me the dry core. "You put a couple of small pieces of punk wood inside those long dog ears, keeping the rain or snow off the punk, and you've got yourself dry tinder. Get a spark next to it…some flint rocks… and you've got yourself a chunk of coal for some fuel." Ray held up the pale gold heart of the scraped-off wood and squeezed it like a sponge. The inside whitened with the pressure, around which so much had crumbled away and left behind fuel waiting to burn.

"Dad used to say the wood was the easy part. Finding the spark was the real challenge."

Grinning, Ray shook a box of matches. "Drawer next to the hooch in the kitchen."

"Matches, punk, bourbon, a magical lake up ahead…we're set. We don't need dog ears to keep the wood warm."

"We got my ears."

"I love your hound-dog ears." I kissed his left one, the one slightly larger than the right and scarred from a fight he got into with some white boys when he was twelve. They pinned his face down on the pavement and dragged him across it. Small scars remained on his cheek and chin, and a small almond-shaped bald spot was near his temple, the follicles too damaged for hair to grow back. It was a June day when he told me about it, we sat in bed, and the outside heat swelled around us. Our air conditioner at the house was on the fritz, being old and having no let-up time between runs. We were prepared to drop a lot of money on

OCTOBER

fixing or replacing it. I sat behind him and massaged his neck. I asked about the scars and the bald spot. He didn't hesitate. Why the fight started and why those boys, who were the same age as him, did what they did didn't surprise me. The reasons were no different before Ray and have been no different after Ray. When the fight was over, one of the four boys—one who had been hiding—ran back and helped Ray up. Blood and skin lay everywhere. Ray limped home, and his mother took care of him. His father vowed vengeance, but his mother voiced it would only make things worse. Simon was the boy who helped Ray. Years later, Ray found him owning a landscaping company. He had reached out to several companies for bids on keeping the hospice grounds. Simon's company won. Ray remembered Simon's red hair, freckles, and soft face. He cried when the other three started in on Ray, and then the other three took their turns attacking both boys. Simon suffered a bloody nose and bruises. The others threatened him if he snitched—and then threatened him for being nothing like them. He ran into the woods and waited for the voices of the other three boys calling out his name and the epithets about his sensitivity to fade with the late afternoon dust. Once when Simon took a break from mowing Blue Sky's lawn, he knocked on Ray's door. He cleared his throat and, before saying anything, broke down in tears under the weight of memory and responsibility for what he did and what he did not do. In the office light they hugged. Ray forgave Simon and the other boys.

"As Christ would do," Ray said as they stood in his office painted like the yellow feathers of a bird when its body seems charged from inside by light. Many years later, Simon was one of the first people to reach out to Ray when he was diagnosed and then to me after he died.

"Punk and dog ears," Ray chuckled. He used the hiking stick to shift his seat on the rock and, as he did, howled like a hound, but seconds in, his voice cracked.

I grabbed the water canteen.

"I guess I need to warm up with that, too. Maybe it's the bourbon. Phew, it's gotten warmer." His eyes watered. "OK. Up we go." The hiking stick warped as he stood. He coughed some more, dusted off his pants, smiled at me, and started walking.

I swung my hips side to side, hoping my back would loosen up and welcome the bourbon needling my veins. On our walks along the Chickataw, before the long days of hospital visits, we stopped to watch the water flow over the rocks. He never strayed too far from me. We waited for each other. But on the trail to the lake, he could have gone on without me with the pace he found again, as though that pace had been buried in him and was now uncovered or it was being used up for perhaps the final time, propelling him onto what could have been any trail in any woods and taking him wherever without me—so far away he would have to wait for me, and not the other way around.

OCTOBER

As we walked over a long hill thick with dirt and rocks, the wind picking up and throwing leaves, Lake Merritt sparkled in front us when we reached the flat stretch of land between the hill and water. Light filled the open space in the ring of trees surrounding the shore—fully grown, saplings, and felled old giants. The day's rising temperature, the layers of my clothes, and our hike had nothing to do with my warmth.

"Left or right?"

My eyes followed the trail rounding along the water's edge disappearing at the opposite shore and squiggling back to where we had stood. "Right," I answered.

"Counterclockwise it is." Ray's finger traced the loop, starting at the imaginary number six of the invisible clock under our feet and circling past the imaginary number three, which was a lump of bare tree branches jutting out from the rest of the woods like a mass of wild hair; up to twelve, which lined up not too far off the noonday sun; then left, over to nine, where shadows gathered between a low patch of gray-brown land and silhouettes of picnic tables and garbage cans; and finished where we stood, completing this motion in one swoop like a fishing line piercing the surface and settling its arc in darkness below.

I grabbed the crook of his elbow when he started forward. "You go. I want to sit here and rest. My feet feel a little swollen." I sat on a stone bench near the trail entrance and, before I did, glimpsed at the words chiseled on the back—WPA 1939. "It's been so long since I've done something like this. Go on." I shooed him on while I took off one of my gloves.

His angle to me pronounced his whiskers and sagging jowl, but the desire inside the brown irises of his eyes had not faded. "I'll just go around the loop, and then we can picnic." He slung the backpack to his side and dropped it on the bench. "If you get out one of those granola bars, watch out for bears."

"Ray?"

He stopped and spun in place.

"Are you taking the hooch?"

His laugh bellowed. "It's in the main pouch." Kissing me on my forehead, he placed the hiking stick next to me, its metal clanging on the stone.

"You don't want that?"

He shook his head no, his lips jutting out. "I'll be back before you know it."

"I'll be waiting with bells on."

He shuffled back onto the trail and crossed the small hump cutting across the dirt. Some birds scattered from the treetops. He didn't stop for anything, not even to look behind and wave at me. He kept going farther down until the land and air absorbed his thinning blue-black shadow. He moved like he used to—without an IV tapped into his arms or a vomit bag tied nearby—and he left so suddenly, not like he was free of me but like the loop around the water held something he had to have. Far away,

OCTOBER

the sun shone on the other side of the lake and behind trees as though a body was meant to go there and surrender itself to the light passing over the water like a face from heaven.

After taking off my hiking shoes and massaging my feet, I sipped the bourbon. A giant tree trunk stood next to me in an open space and must have been one of the biggest before natural forces or human hands whittled it. I cinched up my laces, walked over, and peered over the trunk ringed with centuries' worth of histories. Some of those rings were more prominent than others. Some were thicker or thinner, faded green-gray or more amber. Some had colors as slim as watercolors, and some had nothing more than an outline shaped by the rings coming before and after. With black splotches spread like ink in the wood, some rings looked damaged. But damaged or not, they were all there, unified by the center like a seed split open halfway and, when it was a seed, must have been the size of an eyeball looking upon moments until history rippled its texture into life, holding the sensations of where and when something happened—those moments dying off but also preserved for the next generation of the living to see and return to, always present and maybe hidden but never absent, chronicling life, growing in relation to the long line of a story spiraling out.

Tracing the group of rings closest to me, my fingers moved backward in time, passed over the middle part of decades ago, and ended at the single beginning.

Those rings under my hand had been there before I ever existed, and like a stone overturned and life underneath revealed, those rings vibrated with their histories pushing into the air, soil, and wood and under my palms. I did not know their exact births and deaths, but their earth-tinted chronology spoke to me with events and voices spinning in those rings surviving and, in their after-effects, meant to be inherited. One by one they opened up to me, and one ring told no less of a history than another one.

At that first ring, the woods in the foreground were no different, but there were no cabins, no shuttles or trains to cabins, and no roads leading to those cabins in the background—nothing but trees and birds coming and going with the cycles of the seasons. The lake was bigger, or maybe it was smaller because water started to fill a hole created by the shifting land. No trail existed—no cut-through nor around the body of water—and the seed of that tree trunk and its soon-to-be rings was planted.

Further out from that first ring, trees multiplied, the land shifted more, the water in the lake rose and fell, flowers grew and wilted, animals fed and grazed here and died or were killed by other animals and by the first peoples who lived here—tribes seeing everything connected by breath, spirits, and the shapes of the land underneath the cycles of the sun and the moon. A woman and her child stopped here. The woman let go of the child's hand, and he picked a leaf from a snapped-off tree limb and carried that leaf back to the village where he asked his father

OCTOBER

for a burnt stick and drew around the leaf's edge on animal hides until that single skin was buried over the shoulders of his father who died when, at rings further in, Westward Expansion, Manifest Destiny, and white settlers arrived with their bullets, diseases, machines, and a three-person god, dividing the land.

At another ring, Ray's family began in this country, pulled from Africa in vulgar ships to a coast where they remained chained, beaten, bought, and sold. Through the centuries, the rings growing out from there, their children and their grandchildren survived when finally, several rings later, Ray's grandfather Poppa Julian read the words of Jesus after dinner one night. The room was quiet, and within its walls, everything glowed. He repeated the message of the Golden Rule and talked how soon the time would come when Jesus would descend again to Earth. "They'd been waiting for so long to stand with Him," he said, "and all kin and friends have wanted for so long to have Him place His holy hands upon us and say, 'You are truly free and need not be sad no more.' We had to find a voice in a country never wanting us to have a voice. They did all they could to stop us, and yet our hearts did not grow cold or empty because the Gospels reminded us how much work was left to be done. The meek shall inherit the earth, the first shall be last, the last first, those who hunger will be fed and thirst will be quenched, and those who mourn shall be comforted. Our hearts knew strength was love, hope, patience, and purpose. More than animals, we are men and women, boys and girls, old and young with hearts and minds and souls rich in love, intelligence, and direction. And finally, that day came, the Lord heard us and everyone pleading for a change, for the words of the New Testament to be made flesh, to become more than simply talk to make certain people feel good about themselves without having to live those words inside their skin, and the dark days of slavery were over when people truly listened to His message. But now we are onto another talk, one of economy and money and people, which is no different than the same talk we had not that long ago. Why do some folks turn other folks into nothing more than profits and losses? Truth is, the wealthy don't care nothing 'bout the color of your skin but care every little bit about your contribution to their bank accounts. They are still dividing people. They are still basing people on potential, not love. Why is our desire to walk through life and all our hours on Earth without humiliation such a strange and difficult thing, when, long ago, Christ Himself taught us it didn't have to be that way, we weren't made to be that way, and we were made for something greater and not of this Earth? To be more than someone's deposit or burden of debt! To be more than a price. The one thing that has not, has never changed, never will change is the message of our Lord. To love and to be loved is everything needing remembering."

OCTOBER

A little further out, at another ring, Ray and I exchanged our own rings with the promise "in sickness and in health." We bought the house at another ring. We buried our grandparents and parents. We toyed with the idea of leaving Cole for Taylor. His cancer appeared in a ring whose blackened, bulbous outline nearly erased our words. The mass in his stomach looked like a knot, and that ring was nearest the trunk's edge—the most-recent present. And at the furthest ring, the one closest to me, Cole, the county, the state, the region, the country had changed in many ways and yet in other ways had not changed at all. If I wanted to see a change in the rings, I would have to return there, but I would be either too old to see a moment like that or I would be dead, buried alongside the trunk, rather than next to Ray. I would be part of it all—the slow expanse from a single seed, the weathering of good and bad events, the shedding, the regrowth, the thriving. I was part of it all within sight and touch of everything else.

After tracing the last ring, my fingers fell from it. The rings turned from the past to the present, and in each one, I had heard and saw a way in and a way out. Beyond the ring closest to me hovered an invisible future ring yet to form, a moment with no one in it whom I could see, but the moment had a field filled with stones, trees, a sun, and a voice where, waiting like a message from some other plane of existence relying upon other pieces to fall into place before appearing, told my heart at that tree trunk, in front of all those past rings and histories, I would need a friend in my darkest hours and a friend would find me without me having to ask for one.

On the other side of the lake's trail, Ray's silhouette walked my way. He picked up a few sticks and tree limbs, assessing them in his hands. He was neither a skinny man nor a man weighed down by sickness. The March sun was so high and charged the sky so brightly you could cut swaths from it, roll it into a bolt, and take it home to turn it into a dress for yourself to wear on lonely days or on days when you'd be out on the town and everyone can see you, not to fan jealousy or pride but to display beauty and joy. Ray waved at me, and all the cabins and hikers in the area must have seen his smile. He was returning to me as he promised.

The lake shimmered, and a body could float there long enough to see a day go by, and if I had a coin, before throwing it in the lake, I would wish upon it for mercy and for Ray's health not to be perfect again but to be less of a struggle when the next health scare came along. But I had no coins. I had a backpack full of granola bars and a bottle of bourbon anyone with a fire in their belly would enjoy on such a day, proving the spirit of life may ebb and flow but never ends. I had the water, the land, Ray, and the day in front of us and the days behind us sometimes moving in waves or sometimes floating like a body in water.

OCTOBER

My fingers stopped tracing rings in the tree trunk. "How was it?"

"It's a great little loop." His chest heaved up and down as he panted. He drank from the canteen for several seconds. Staring at the lake, he said, "Would be fun to get in there."

"Would be a bit chilly."

If the weather were warmer, the clouds breaking over the surface, we would be in our swimsuits. Ray would lumber into the water before me, his arms sturdy in the air until his waist submerged—they would drop like wings. It would be the middle of summer, it would be hot and humid, but swimming would cool us off. I would wade in after him, after adjusting my swim cap, which I never liked wearing because of all the curls to tuck under it, like placing a beanie atop a sagebrush. I would follow him into that large circle of blue where he waited for me and where we would float with the breeze rolling over us and through the leaves, birds scattering all around, and the day too long to become night. The water's dark blue would lift away the scars on his body. We would splash around without worrying about anything.

"I'm famished." He patted his tummy before scrambling up a pile of rocks and felled trees.

"What are you doing?"

"This is as big as a headstone. Smooth on one side, too. Real smooth. You could put it all on here. Name, date, one of those sayings. Maybe some angel wings right there." He pointed to a gray-white ribbon near the bottom of the stone. "Better yet, we could put it in the garden at the cabin."

"We'd have to get permission from the owners."

"They wouldn't know."

"If it's a headstone, they will."

"It's not a headstone. I was making a comparison." He tried picking it up. "We could take it back to Cole."

"We can't take that back. It should stay here."

The large stone clumped on the ground, and on his way down, he slipped and skinned his knee. Blood soaked his pants as he hobbled around.

"Raymond! Are you OK?" I offered the metal hiking stick.

His eyes passing over the leaves and grass, he grabbed a stick. It was nearly three quarters as tall as him and, the way he gazed at it, held him more than he held it. He nodded, but not to me, and tested the stick by leaning his weight onto it. It absorbed him. "This'll work." He tapped the stick on the grass and dirt.

"You want to carry that back?"

He thumped the stick between us. "Yes. Very much so." He tightened both hands around it. His hands relaxed when we ate lunch, but his eyes on the stick did not.

∙ ∙ ∙

OCTOBER

The cabin was dark when we returned. Several hours had passed, and the sun burned a thin orange line behind the trees. We opened the door, and the smells we left greeted us like they had been waiting for us to sit down at the table once again. Cedar and pine wafted over us. Ray flipped on the lights, walked into the kitchen, and poured glasses of wine.

"Do you like all this?" he asked.

"Yes."

"Everything?"

"Everything."

"It was so great to get out today. We haven't done something like that in some time."

"Now we can relax." I stretched my legs over him on the couch.

He untied my hiking shoes and dropped them to the floor. His face scrunched. "If you weren't sweaty, I'd massage them."

"Next time."

"We should get back to the Chickataw. If I can handle this, that'll be nothing."

His voice was so declarative it shocked me, speaking as though a peak had come and gone and anything and everything after that peak was all downhill with a breeze at its back.

"Are you going to mail those?" I nodded at his letters on the desk.

"There's a box down at the end of the drive. If not now, when we get back."

He stood up, cracked his back, and stepped outside the front door. He came back with the stick he found at the lake. He spun it in his hands and, returning to the couch, angled it against him like a flag he was responsible for displaying anywhere he and its colors went—into battle or peace or to symbolize a person, place, moment, or thing—but the flag was missing, and everything remaining was the post on which it flew and marked the ground. He found the remote and turned on the music.

After the first bars of the piano's intro, he said, "I almost died, Patty."

"When? Today?"

"On the surgery table. I laid there and believed I was dead. I heard the doctors. I heard the heart monitor. They moved around me with their scalpels. The doctors and nurses kept talking, but I couldn't answer them. My mouth was frozen. Everything was frozen except for that light everyone talks about appeared. It got bigger and brighter like an eye opening."

"Why didn't you tell me this?"

Spinning the stick in his hands, he shrugged.

"You didn't die."

"No, I didn't." He knocked the stick on the living room rug twice, which echoed throughout the cabin. A saxophone solo softened the song on the speakers. "This place is great. Cozy.

OCTOBER

Trees. The lake. Imagine all four seasons up here. We could be here for a long time."

"But it's not our home. It's our get-away. We could pick a season. I'm willing to do that."

"But it could be our home."

"We need to focus on the here and now. We have no idea about the future."

"I'm healthy. We're here. We'll be back in Cole before you know it, and we can decide then."

"We can't keep pretending things'll get better. They can change, Ray. I don't think coming up here for good is a good idea."

"It would be."

"I don't want us to skirt around anything. Your cancer can come back. The doctors said so."

He wrinkled his forehead, squished his lips, and spun the stick counterclockwise.

I broke the long silence. "Why don't we get cleaned up. I'll start dinner. I'll jump in the shower and wash my feet."

"You go ahead. I'm going to put this in the shed. I'll start dinner when I get back in." He stood and headed for the shed.

The blue-black glow of the land outside the windows hovered around the shed where, when Ray reached it, the light clicked on. He moved some things around and set the stick across two old paint cans on the workbench. Standing with his hands on his hips, he stared down at the stick. His silhouette moved inside the shed's light, determined to start something he had no choice but to finish.

The bathroom tile chilled my bare wet feet. I dried my hair and wrapped my robe around me before entering the bedroom and slipping into my comfy clothes. My soreness had increased since we got back from our hike. I wanted to fade away with relaxation into the rest of the night and with another glass of wine and some chocolate.

On my way to the living room, I stopped between the bathroom and bedroom. Singing echoed from the kitchen where Ray stood. The shed's light broke through the cabin and its curtains. Ray shuffled from refrigerator to counter and cradled sweet potatoes, a tub of butter, and chicken. A mixing bowl gleamed on the counter. For a moment, my heart jumped because rather than seeing him in the cabin's kitchen I saw him in the kitchen in our house in Cole.

He rocked back and forth at his knees, head down, and his hum worked its way into words to a spiritual from his family's church. He sang about the Jordan River, its water cleansing people stepping into it, never sweeping them away or pulling them under. He turned his head up and faced the kitchen windows and, behind its curtains, the shed. The sunset lowered some more. He sang with no effort. Whatever was in him flowed out of his body and was more than merely his breath.

OCTOBER

I hadn't heard him sing in so long. His voice remained raspy from the chemo—his voice of living after nearly dying. Hearing his song took me from a place I had been to a place I have often thought about where folks, after having wandered from what they knew, can come to a rest and be confident they have nowhere else to go.

And then his voice wavered holding the last note as long as his body allowed, surrendering everything it had to give. He shook when he finished. His chest heaved. His back arched. He looked up as though a warm light spread down on him for the eternal requests lingering in his song he sang like a prayer.

With me hiding in the shadows and in the song's echoes, Ray diced the sweet potatoes, cubed the butter, and placed the chicken on the cooking sheet. He cleaned the knife. He set the oven and, grabbing the pen and pad of paper from the desk, kicked out the recliner. He dozed off before I entered the living room and before the moonrise overtook the sunset.

After dinner, we cleaned dishes, and I watched TV. Ray scrabbled around in the shed. The stick lay like an altar on the paint cans. Metal scraped. Wood snapped. He came in for some coffee.

"How's it going?"

"I'd like to take some of those trees out in the back, piece them together, and make a long table…bigger than this one." His chin jabbed at the kitchen table. "Can you smell pine in here? It would be perfect. *This long table.*" His voice faded like a sailor about to describe a journey thriving in his imagination. "We can have a whole lot of people sitting at it with us for a long, long time. Bill and Sheila could be our first guests."

I tightened the blanket around me because of the draft from the back door, smiled, and held back tears when I smelled the pine and saw new friends sitting at that table decorated with candles, fine linen napkins, and silverware. But those scene's vapors were so far in front of me they could not harden into reality.

"What about the stick?" I asked.

"A ragged piece of wood right now, but it'll be something good before you know it. There's something else inside waiting to come out. All that other stuff around it doesn't matter. Don't wait up for me." He kissed my forehead and stepped back into the shed.

I barely saw him through Friday and Saturday. He banged around out there, tools buzzed, followed by long moments of silence. His silhouette, cast by sun or moon, moved back and forth against the cabin's curtains.

I finished Gloria's novel, and my options on the shelves were biographies, romances, thrillers, horrors, westerns, and the stuffy stuff that wins awards and sounds important but most folks don't read because the authors don't know how to tell a story. The stacks of magazines were a few months old and were mostly

OCTOBER

about country living or hosting small parties at home—being a good hostess, one no friend could forget and, more importantly, no stranger could forget because he or she, by being invited and cared for by the host, was no longer a stranger but another friend added to the ever-growing group. Ray and I had hosted parties mainly during the big holidays, the major college-football bowls, and my interest since childhood, the running for the Triple Crown. But, standing in the cabin and seeing the potential Ray imagined, part of me wanted to host more—there was something communal about it, making sure everyone knows everyone at the party, providing good food and drinks, and enjoying laughter and all the different kinds of folks who make a community. Not that our parties were high-society soirees or I was a matriarch gracing my people with my presence and offering food and drink my staff of chefs and bartenders prepared. No, the parties Ray and I held were blue jeans, flannel shirts, khakis, some dresses and dress shirts, cowboy hats, trucker hats, no hats, nice hair, big hair, uncooperative hair, no hair, and jobs ranging from teachers to shop workers to my colleagues at the library to Ray's colleagues at the hospice to the recently unemployed or those stars-in-their-eyes folks who found their calling, not a career, and were either ready to make the jump into the unknown or had reached its precipice.

 For the two days Ray was in the shed, clouds rolled in, and the light was an unwavering bright gray. He did not appear for lunch or dinner and told me to set meals outside the shed. He peed behind the shed, and I waited for a knock on the cabin's front door from neighbors who weren't too happy about seeing Ray relieve himself outside. But no knock came.

"Honey," I started to say, standing in the space between the back door and the shed.

"I'm looking for that box with masking tape on it. Black tape. Those others over there are brown tape. I need the black-taped one." He moved a cardboard tube that nearly hit me in the head. "It's got cans of stains in it. The tape kept the lid shut."

"Do you need the stains now?"

"I'm gonna need it."

When he slid over boxes of motor oil, the stick from our hike appeared from one of the shed's corners. He had whittled the top, which looked like an animal gnawed it, but cloth wrapped the body of the stick.

"It's our last night here. Come to bed. Things'll be here tomorrow."

"We're leaving tomorrow. Won't have time."

"You can be out there first thing in the morning. None of that's going anywhere. I'll make us your favorite breakfast, put some coffee in you, and you can be out here until we leave."

He stopped rummaging around and panted, pale and tired.

"I can help you look for things, move things, if you want."

OCTOBER

He flopped on a plastic bucket. "It's dusty. Your nose won't like it." He coughed, and the cough sounded like when the tube first came out at the hospital and not enough water soothed his throat.

"Come to bed, Ray. It's late. None of this will change overnight. There's some strawberry-pretzel salad waiting for you."

"Found it!" He planted a kiss on my lips and, after lifting a box, tore off its masking tape. "Lots of options." Cans clanked on the shed floor. "Blonde. Ash. Cherry. Walnut. And this one." He held one by its handle. "But it might be too dark. It would look like the stick got stuck in a fire and no one pulled it out in time."

I didn't tell him most of the cans had expired.

"*This* is the one." He pulled out another can.

"Clear?"

He set down the can next to the stick. "When I started carving, just to see what was inside, the wood here has this gold to it." He pulled the stick from the shed's corner. The cloth wrapping its body turned in his chapped palms. "No need to cover it up." He cracked open the can and dipped a brush. "That color is too pretty. Just seal it. I'm bringing it back with us. Wet or dry. I'm bringing it back."

"I guess it won't take up much space on the train."

"I'll carry it. They can charge me extra if they throw a fit."

I looked at the stick and then at Ray concentrating on his brush strokes. The stain's aroma hit me right away. I covered my face with my shirt collar. "You should wear a mask."

"I'm gonna finish this before we leave. Stain and all. Everything about it."

Sunday came, and he had yet to emerge from the shed. I glanced outside the curtains and couldn't see him. The shed door was open, the light was on, but nobody was in there. I rushed outside and followed a little trail of shoe marks in the soft ground and remaining snow. He sat on a large rock by the side of the cabin, hands crossed at his wrists that rested on a dense cane half the height of him, its top, were he to stand up, ending at his hips. The cane was so clear-coated that the grain and the gold underbelly, the wood exposed from his carving, shone through the transparent skin as though black dirt had been pushed off glass and beneath that glass the sun shone.

Turning to me, morning on his face, his gravelly voice said, "Hello, Patty Girl."

"Well, I do declare." I kissed him. "You finished?"

"It is done." He turned the stick to where he carved numbers and words in the body.

"That date is today," I said.

He nodded.

"COLE – LAKE MERRITT – COLE," I repeated the phrase next to the date.

OCTOBER

"Out and back." His stained fingers ran over the places and direction carved in the wood. "When we get back is when this thing starts its life. Look here." He rolled the main section over. The date and the places disappeared. His name and a phrase appeared on the other side.

"RAYMOND CHARLES PEMBERTON MADE THIS WITH HIS WIFE PATTY BY HIS SIDE," I read aloud.

"I wanted to add AND IT TOOK EVERYTHING THEY HAD, but there was not enough room or time. My hands cramped up, and all that small space and dust got to me. I got as far as I did."

The sun rose higher, glancing our shoulders and necks.

"Breakfast is ready," I said.

"I want to be here for a little more."

I rubbed the beard he hadn't shaved since we left home. I hadn't remembered it being so white.

We went inside and ate. Other than mumbling how good everything tasted or remarking on something small we would miss from the cabin or our trip, we were quiet. His hands were chapped, and flakes of wood clung to his sweater. The table for the kitchen he had envisioned was not physical, yet it stood there with us. I saw it and the light pouring in from the windows behind the curtains. The table's wood glowed like water inside a glass bowl on a bright day. Ray sat at that table, his back to me, but no one else was there, not the friends he talked about or the neighbors we had met in the area. It was just him in a light clearing the sky and expanding inside a room because it had no other choice until it changed a season and all the living things in it, faded away, and would return when it needed to be seen again.

We cleaned the cabin and gathered our things. The van idled in the driveway outside. The driver stepped out—the same man who shuttled us up.

"My husband is on his way." I glanced over my shoulder at where we ate, slept, and played and at the landscape and the shed before closing the curtains. Standing in front of it, the sun and the moon and Ray moved to and from the shed, but that window never moved and was clear enough to look out or to be seen from.

The driver took some items from my hand and helped me into the seat.

After a few minutes, Ray came around the cabin from the back. He held his cane. Stopping between the cabin's front door and the van, he turned and breathed deeply several times. The driver offered to help him into the van, but Ray brushed him off and used his cane.

Our train pulled out of the Tubersville station and chugged toward Cole.

Squeezing my hand, Ray said, "I had a great time. Thank you. Where to next?"

"Let's get home first before anything else."

OCTOBER

On the way down from the mountains, within those hours we had left, we held each other. The tree trunks thinned, but their new buds thickened, the snow disappeared, and the lower-third of the mountains flourished into greens as the valley spread out, leading to the highway and its exit for Cole. So much of what we saw on the way down had not been there on the way up. Spring had arrived, and heading into it, we had not missed it.

I drove us home. Ray was too tired and had to stop a few times. New aches. New pains. Was his nose bloody from the elevation and cold air—maybe all that time spent in the shed with its dust, stains, and carvings? Or had something formed in his body? He used his cane every time he stepped in and out of the car, inside and around our house, and everywhere in Cole before returning to the hospital in Taylor. But of all the loves we reminisced about during the months we were home and when he relapsed, the greatest of those was our destination.

10

When an ambulance's siren and engine scream by the house, I rub my eyes and look at the computer's clock. Almost midnight. I dozed off for a while, making a nest in my mind, and missed the moon brightening the sky. The curtains glow, and Ray's cane is as silent as it's been and yet full of words so quiet only I hear them.

All the children have floated through the neighborhood and up and down Cole, taking all the candy Davis, Karen, and I and our neighbors set out. And it wouldn't surprise me much if some parents decided to help themselves to our stash. You can't walk through a night like this empty-handed without some help by your side. When school returns Monday, sitting still at a desk will be more challenging than the assignments, I reckon. Teachers will have to block out most of the day for recess and get those children outside to burn off as much sugar as possible. And with Thanksgiving coming up and Santa on his way, these sugar highs are just the beginning of riding waves.

The air stills once more, and the night returns to quiet when the ambulance reaches the end of Ashbery Street, where it will

OCTOBER

turn on Cornell Lane and speed over the hills toward Cole General.

As soon as I rock forward in my chair and turn off the desk lamp, the message icon on my computer screen flickers behind the photo of Ray and me at the cabin.

<Hey there sorry for silence. Better late than never right?>

I stare at it and then the power button. A shadow flutters behind the curtains and breaks up the moonlight streaking the fabric. I stand up, head into the kitchen, and pour myself some water to wash down an aspirin. My costume drapes over Davis and Karen's stools. Darkness patches the rest of the house. No more cars drive by outside. Without me inside them, my frazzled wig and white-sheet dress look like a ghost ready to inflate once it finds a host.

The message icon blinks again.

<You there? You up? I know it's not too late for you unless you've changed your routine. I got a quick burst of coffee in me to hold me over until sunrise. Don't ask me why. Maybe because I can't believe the year is almost gone.>

I stand in front of the computer, bracing myself on the chair.

<Anyway here's that translation to the photo I sent you a while back and promised to get to you. My friend was able to get her grandma to help out. She lived in over there in that area when she was younger before coming to this country. She knows the language like the back of her hand. More like riding a bike. You

never forget. Thought you still might want to read it and see it alongside the photo. My friend says her grandma's translation is as close as it can get without being literal and losing "poetic truth" which she says is more important. She and her grandma say this. Looking over it and reading it again and again myself I agree. Maybe it all makes sense now. It does to me even though I got an idea what the words were about just by looking at the photo. Seems like a no-brainer. Pretty clear from a distance with bad eyes and glasses as big as bottles as my grandpa would say. I've read it so many times I'm starting to memorize it. Maybe it's all this coffee LOL! It's just much more powerful now for me. I bet it will be for you too.>

I save the translation, placing it inside the computer folder marked SAUL.

Another message covers Ray.

<You there?>

After several minutes of me standing, watching, he types again. <OK, well, I bet you're sound asleep after your favorite holiday with your neighbors. Another big one this year? Go all out again? Tell them I said hi and I can't wait to meet them when I get to make it out there to y'all. We'll have lots of fun. I'll take us all out for dinner and ice cream. We'll see all your places. I saw on the weather you had a good clear night for tonight. I'm jealous. How many witches showed up? Any zombies? The Night of the Living Dead is a classic, still is. A horde of the undead is

OCTOBER

worse than a single one headed your way. No one comes out my way for any of that stuff you and your neighbors do. If they do, they're out for some cow tipping or snipe hunting or underage drinking and You Know What in the backseat of a car! Who can blame them? You got to get away to come back different. Got to run now. My coffee is calling. I've been real busy but would love to talk when things settle down. Hope you're doing real good. Let's catch up soon. Love, Saul.>

His cursor disappears, replaced by Ray next to me in our photo. The moon has moved a bit behind the curtains. I turn off the computer and finish getting ready for bed.

But after reading a bit, I can't fall asleep. I return to the desk and turn on the computer. I do not yawn, wobble in place, question my surroundings, or blink my eyes to erase whatever illusions are sometimes there at certain hours. I slip on my glasses and open Saul's folder.

Alongside his photo, I click on the translation for the inscription on the base of the cross.

> THE DRAGON SITS BY THE SIDE OF THE ROAD
> AND WATCHES THOSE WHO PASS.
> BEWARE, LEST THE DRAGON DEVOUR YOU.
> WE TRAVEL TO THE FATHER OF OUR SOULS,
> AND IT IS NECESSARY TO PASS THE DRAGON.
> —ST. CYRIL OF JERUSALEM

WILLIAM AUTEN

    The photo turns to me and completes its message in the field of stone markers; blacks, grays, and whites; and the words tying together Earth, bodies, and sky while the people who had been alive fill the points between birth and death. Their faces and figures continue moving with me, and their moments reach out from a past that doesn't move but extends past its course. Reading the translation with the photo is like reading a book for the second time but with a different pair of eyes that had a hunch but could not confirm it until later. I part the curtains slightly to look out the window. I look around my apartment, at the photo, and the translation. What I know about an end and a beginning is wrong. The curtains fall closed.

    I open a new document and create a list of people I haven't talked to in a while, starting with Ray's kids and siblings at the top. I open my letter to Saul, revise its beginning, delete the rest but put it back in, return to the beginning, and stop there for now.

> Thank you for the translation and the image. You're right: They are so powerful together, and they mean so much to me, especially coming from you. Thank you for thinking of me. I can't begin to tell you how happy I am to hear from you. It's been quite a month for me, and I'd love to tell you all about it when there's time.

    I peel back the curtains—a quarter moon, not the full moon perfect for this time of year. The washed-out background of

OCTOBER

Saul's photo and the translation glow on the computer. Everything in my apartment is in its place, and I am back among it and am not confused, lost, or wondering where I have to go. Everyone else in my neck of the woods is asleep, and I will see them tomorrow and will be with them until, by choice or circumstance, we can no longer be next to each other. The photo of Ray and me at the cabin is as bright as the moonlight reaching me on the cusp of a new day and a new month, drawing closer to a new year behind curtains I will open in the morning, as I have done as I long as I've been here.

ACKNOWLEDGMENTS

Thank you to everyone who contributed to this novel and thank you for reading and supporting my work. And Nick, you got your dragon.

ABOUT THE AUTHOR

William Auten is the author of the novels *In Another Sun* and *Pepper's Ghost* and the short-story collection *A Fine Day Will Burn Through*. His work has appeared widely in print and online. williamauten.com

www.ingramcontent.com/pod-product-compliance
Lightning Source LLC
Chambersburg PA
CBHW022033290426
44109CB00014B/853